PRAYERS
— for Men —

★ ★ ★

PRAYERS
for Men
★ ★ ★

BARBOUR BOOKS
An Imprint of Barbour Publishing, Inc.

© 2020 by Barbour Publishing, Inc.

Compiled by Tracy Sumner

Written by Tracy Sumner and John Hudson Tiner

ISBN 978-1-64352-336-1

Text compiled from *Daily Wisdom for Men* collections, published by Barbour Publishing, Inc.

Published by Barbour Books, an imprint of Barbour Publishing, Inc., 1810 Barbour Drive, Uhrichsville, Ohio 44683, www.barbourbooks.com

Our mission is to inspire the world with the life-changing message of the Bible.

Member of the
Evangelical Christian
Publishers Association

Printed in China.

INTRODUCTION

One of the greatest privileges you as a follower of Jesus Christ have is that of prayer—actually communicating with God, the Creator of the Universe, in a personal, loving way. Your gracious heavenly Father *invites* you to talk with Him—to confess your sins, to plead for His favor on those you love, to help You live in the power He has for you as one of His beloved children. . .the list goes on and on.

Those, and many others, are just the kinds of prayers you'll find in *Everyday Prayers for Men*.

This practical, encouraging, easy-to-follow book packs a powerful dose of inspiration into just a few short minutes of reading each day. In each entry, you'll find:

- A scripture passage on which to meditate
- A just-right-sized devotional prayer

Each of the prayers in this book can meet you right where you are. . .and also motivate and inspire you toward deeper communication with your loving heavenly Father. So as you read each day's scripture and prayers, be ready to be blessed—and also amazed that such a big God actually wants to hear from you and communicate with you.

THE BLESSED LIFE

*Blessed is the man who walks not in the counsel
of the ungodly, nor stands in the path of sinners,
nor sits in the seat of the scornful; but his delight
is in the law of the Lord, and in His law
he meditates day and night.*

PSALM 1:1-2 NKJV

Father of all blessings, every day I encounter ideas
and philosophies that try to compete with You and
Your written Word for my attention. At best, these
things are worldly distractions; at worst, they directly
contradict what You have said. Please help me to stay
focused on the blessed promises, commandments,
and encouragements in the Bible. Lord, make me hungrier every day for Your Word. Help me to make Bible
reading and meditation as much a part of my day as
eating, drinking, and breathing.

A SENSE OF WONDER

*Ye are our epistle written in our hearts,
known and read of all men.*

2 CORINTHIANS 3:2 KJV

Lord, Your Word is a light that guides me to righteousness. It contains wonderful poetry and soul-stirring songs. I read in it exciting stories of heroes of the faith. I marvel at its miraculous events, almost beyond human comprehension. Each day of reading the Bible is a new adventure and a wonderful journey.

I pray, Father, that I will always have a sense of wonder when I read Your Word, that it will always be fresh and illuminate my life. I pray that I will read Your Word, contemplate Your message, and keep it in my mind throughout each day.

SAVED TO SERVE

The righteous care about justice for the poor,
but the wicked have no such concern.

PROVERBS 29:7 NIV

Generous God, my heart breaks for those who don't have enough to live their lives— sufficient food, proper housing, enough money to pay for utilities. . .the list, sadly enough, goes on and on. Your Word teaches me that one evidence I have of Your Spirit living in me is my concern for the poor and mistreated. I've trusted You for salvation through Jesus Christ, and I am concerned. Now I ask You to motivate and empower me to serve others. Lord, help me to be ever mindful of those in difficult life situations—and alert for opportunities to serve.

BOLD TYPE

And now, Lord, behold their threatenings:
and grant unto thy servants, that with all
boldness they may speak thy word.
ACTS 4:29 KJV

Lord, when I try to interpret contracts, I must puzzle through the meaning of the jargon, and I struggle with the small type. I wish the text were in large, bold letters, written in simple, easily understood language.

Father, I am like that fine print. I try to conceal my true self from others. Rather than speaking up as a Christian and taking a stand on the pressing issues of the day, I talk around the subjects and make my messages obscure because I do not have the boldness to speak plainly. Father, I pray that my life will be like bold type so people will definitely understand that I am on the side of righteousness.

THE DANGER OF GREED

*The greedy stir up conflict, but those
who trust in the LORD will prosper.*
PROVERBS 28:25 NIV

Provider God, I know that You bless hard work, and I know that You want me to provide my family with the things they need in this life. You are not against financial prosperity, but You are against the sin of greed. You even warn that those who engage in greed put their eternal souls at peril. Your Word tells me to place my trust in You and Your promises of provision. When I truly do that, there is no place in my heart for greed. Lord, You are my protector and provider—I ask You to teach me to trust in You and not in my own striving for financial riches, lest I fall into the sin of greed.

Day 6

═══ **ATTACKING PROBLEMS** ═══

And the Lord shall deliver me from
every evil work, and will preserve me
unto his heavenly kingdom.
2 TIMOTHY 4:18 KJV

Lord, sometimes I look at problems out of the corner of my eye and pretend they are not there. I choose to ignore them, and they grow more serious because of my inattention. Whether they are big or small, I pray that I will accept challenges with a willing heart that will give me a greater chance of success.

Help me attack problems before they attack me. At times, it appears victory is a tiny island in a vast sea of trials. Sometimes I fail, but help me accept failure as an opportunity to try again with more experience. I pray that I will achieve worthy goals while changing for the better.

BEING A GIANT-SLAYER

*Then David said to the Philistine, "You come
to me with a sword, with a spear, and with a
javelin. But I come to you in the name of the
LORD of hosts, the God of the armies of
Israel, whom you have defied."*

1 SAMUEL 17:45 NKJV

Mighty God, the young shepherd David needed Your
help to slay a literal giant. I need Your help to slay some
figurative giants. Sometimes I face life situations that
are just too big for me to handle in my own strength.
From where I stand, issues with my family, job, and
ministry can look overwhelming. But I know that with
You at my side, I can slay any of these giants. Thank
You, Lord, that while I can't accomplish anything
for You in my own strength, *with* You I can do anything!

Day 8

DOING GOOD

*Who is going to harm you if you are eager
to do good? But even if you should suffer for
what is right, you are blessed. "Do not fear
their threats; do not be frightened."*

1 PETER 3:13–14 NIV

Father in heaven, I am eager to do what is right in
Your eyes. Make me even more so. I want to bless You
and other people through my actions. Please show
me how. Help me to look past my fear of suffering for
doing what is right and instead focus on You and the
blessings You promise for obedience. Make it all about
loving You and other people, and not about fear. Lord,
I commit myself to doing good for You and for others,
and to leaving the results in Your hands.

WHEN AN ENEMY FALLS

Do not gloat when your enemy falls;
when they stumble, do not let your heart rejoice,
or the LORD will see and disapprove and
turn his wrath away from them.
PROVERBS 24:17–18 NIV

Lord, I confess that I'm tempted to feel at least a twinge of joy when a business adversary, a political leader I don't like, or some other opponent falls. That's especially true when that person has treated me in a way I don't think is right. Jesus, You told Your followers to pray for their enemies, not to wish ill on them. Please guard my heart from feeling pleasure or joy when my adversaries suffer or fail. Instead, remind me to pray for those people at all times, knowing that You will deal with them as You see fit.

THE IMPOSSIBLE

And he said, The things which are
impossible with men are possible with God.
LUKE 18:27 KJV

★ ★ ★

Father, some goals do appear unattainable to me. Yet, I see that even what was impossible a few hundred years ago has become possible today: steamships, ocean liners, airplanes, rockets to the moon, instant communication, satellite television, and cell phones were all once considered wildly fanciful, impractical— or basically impossible. If these things can be done with the natural abilities You have given us, how much more is possible when You equip us to act in spiritual matters! Father, help me to never hesitate to begin a good work because it appears unlikely to succeed. Help me remember that I am not acting alone. You are at my side. Dear Lord, give me a faith that learns to trust You more each day.

HUMBLE BEGINNINGS

*Then the LORD took me as I followed
the flock, and the LORD said to me,
"Go, prophesy to My people Israel."*
AMOS 7:15 NKJV

Father God, You don't always use the most highly educated or credentialed men to accomplish Your purposes. Instead, You often choose men of the most humble backgrounds. I think of Amos, a farmer, and Moses, a shepherd. Then there was the carpenter Joseph, the man You chose to be Jesus' earthly father. And the apostles Peter, James, and John were all fishermen. You use the humble, the willing, and those who have the courage and faith to say, "I'm here and available, Lord. Use me as You will!" Though I may not have an impressive background, I know you can do the same with me.

CALLING ON GOD

The LORD is close to all who call on him,
yes, to all who call on him in truth.

PSALM 145:18 NLT

Loving Father, sometimes I feel a deeper need than usual to cling to the promise of Psalm 145:18. You tell me that You're near me when I call, but sometimes it doesn't feel that way. I don't enjoy those times when I feel like You're distant—but I also know those times are valuable because they cause me to look inside myself to make sure I'm calling on You "in truth." Lord, I call out to You today, believing the promise that You will draw close to anyone who calls on You from a pure heart. Thank You for Your love and for Your promise to stay close to me.

═══ CONFIDENT REQUESTS ═══

*This is the confidence we have in approaching God:
that if we ask anything according to his will, he hears
us. And if we know that he hears us—whatever we
ask—we know that we have what we asked of him.*

1 JOHN 5:14–15 NIV

Generous Father, Your Word tells me that You want to bless me, that You want me to have what I ask for in prayer. But You won't give me just anything I request—I must pray according to Your will as it is spelled out in scripture. When I know that what I'm praying for is Your will for me, I can approach You and pray with confidence, knowing that You want to do what I ask. Thank You, Lord, for giving me Your Word so that I can pray according to Your will.

DISCIPLINE:
IT'S FOR YOUR OWN GOOD

My son, do not despise the LORD's discipline, and do not resent his rebuke, because the LORD disciplines those he loves, as a father the son he delights in.
PROVERBS 3:11–12 NIV

Loving Father, no one enjoys being disciplined, even when it's just a simple reprimand. I didn't enjoy it as a boy, and I don't enjoy it as a fully grown man. But You tell me that You discipline me out of Your love and delight for me. So discipline me, Lord. Reprove me when I need it, and help me to endure the reproof with the joy of knowing that it's for my own good. I probably won't enjoy it, but I welcome it—since it causes me to grow and mature in my faith, which in turn glorifies You.

LOVING UNITY

*Can two walk together,
except they be agreed?*
AMOS 3:3 KJV

★ ★ ★

Dear Lord, I am disheartened to encounter disagreement among those who profess to believe in You: fractured denominations, split congregations, and individuals who no longer speak to one another. We should be pulling together. Unfortunately, I confess that because of my own obstinacy, I have contributed to the lack of harmony.

Lord, I pray that I will be more agreeable, that I will not be arrogant or unreasonable. Guide me to choose the right words that will lead to a better walk with You and with my brothers and sisters in Christ. Remind me that even if I am right, I can still be wrong if my comments are not wrapped in love.

THE MEASURE OF A MAN

*Better is the poor who walks in his integrity than
one perverse in his ways, though he be rich.*
PROVERBS 28:6 NKJV

Lord, in this world, people often judge a man by what
he earns or possesses. Those with the biggest bank
accounts and houses are seen as the ones to be ad-
mired. But You don't measure a man like that. You see
into my heart and are most concerned that I am a man
of integrity, that my thoughts and behavior reflect You
in every way. You love integrity! Thank You, Father, that
You don't measure me in terms of what I earn, what I
own, or what I've accomplished. Instead, You measure
me in terms of the good character You've instilled in me.

THE GENUINE ARTICLE

*Whatsoever things are true, whatsoever things
are honest, whatsoever things are just, whatsoever
things are pure, whatsoever things are lovely,
whatsoever things are of good report. . .
think on these things.*
PHILIPPIANS 4:8 KJV

Father, I can see in my daily activities how people
strive for simple perfection: a mathematical proof that
solves a problem in the least number of steps, a musical
composition without a discordant note, a work of art
that achieves harmony and symmetric composition.

Dear Lord, I strive for a life in tune with Your
orchestration. I know that to have an honorable life,
I must be meticulous in eliminating the inferior elements You bring to my attention and strive to reflect
Your higher nature. I want to be a genuine Christian.
I put my life in Your hands so that I can come closer
to reaching that goal.

★ RICHES FROM HEAVEN ★

*Charge them that are rich in this world,
that they be not highminded, nor trust in
uncertain riches, but in the living God,
who giveth us richly all things to enjoy.*

1 TIMOTHY 6:17 KJV

Almighty Father of all creation, I look around and see the good things You have provided. I realize everything comes from You, even my ability to earn a living. When I give back my small offering and reflect on the blessings that You have given me, I cannot help but say, "Thank You, Lord, for letting me use the rest."

Yes, Lord, I understand that the congregation requires this voluntary contribution for its Christian activities in my community. I give it for that purpose in part, but more importantly, I use it to express my gratitude for the spiritual and material blessings I enjoy every day.

SPREADING THE GOOD NEWS

How beautiful upon the mountains are the feet of him that bringeth good tidings, that publisheth peace; that bringeth good tidings of good, that publisheth salvation; that saith unto Zion, Thy God reigneth!

Isaiah 52:7 kjv

Father, when I trace on a map the journeys of Jesus and the apostles, I realize that they must have been rugged individuals to withstand the rigors of their travels. Considering that their mode of transportation was usually walking, they must have been physically strong.

My feet are not dusty and callused like theirs, and I don't have the endurance for a long-distance trek, but I do pray for the spiritual strength to live an overcoming life. On my journey with You, Lord, commission me with joy and perseverance to go forth and proclaim the Good News of salvation.

CREATIVE EFFORT

A faithful man shall abound with
blessings: but he that maketh haste
to be rich shall not be innocent.
PROVERBS 28:20 KJV

Father, I must take prudent risks in my business and personal life. I must be willing to enter new ventures even if success is not certain. However, I should not participate in risky ventures such as gambling. Convenience stores and other outlets sell lottery tickets, and across the country are glitzy casinos.

Help me recognize them for what they are—get-rich-quick schemes that rely on luck rather than You. Help me build my life on creative efforts and useful skills. Prevent me from being enticed into a gambler's way of thinking.

WORRY

*Which of you by taking thought
can add one cubit unto his stature?*
MATTHEW 6:27 KJV

Father, thanks for calming my agitation in times of distress. With Your peace, I smile at my foolish concerns: some situations are already passed and cannot be changed; others were unlikely to happen; some were trivial and not worth my emotional energy—but worry turned a small concern into a long shadow. I could have changed only a few of the situations that troubled me.

Divine Father, equip me to deal with the problems over which I can make a difference. I pray that I will see my troubles more clearly with Your wisdom.

SEEING GOD AS HE IS

*Return to the LORD your God, for he is gracious
and compassionate, slow to anger and abounding
in love, and he relents from sending calamity.*
JOEL 2:13 NIV

Righteous God, You identify Yourself in the Bible as a
holy God who does not tolerate sin. But that's only part
of who You are. You are also a gracious, loving heavenly
Father who extends compassion and patience to me.
Father, I confess that I don't always see the complete
picture of who You really are. You are perfect in Your
holiness, and You must deal with my sin. But You are
also perfect in Your love, so You offer me mercy and
forgiveness. Lord, help me to keep sight of You as
You are: as a holy and righteous God but also as my
gracious, compassionate, loving heavenly Father.

LITTLE THINGS

*Behold also the ships, which though they
be so great, and are driven of fierce winds,
yet are they turned about with a very small
helm, whithersoever the governor listeth.*

JAMES 3:4 KJV

★ ★ ★

Father, when I first came to You I was so determined
to do great works that I considered little jobs beneath
my effort. When I fell short of my goals, I despaired of
ever doing anything for You. All along, a multitude of
small deeds have been available, but I ignored them.
Lord, grant me eyes to see tasks that need to be done
and a willing heart to do them. In Your name, I ask Your
help in using my daily activities to show kindness and
concern for others.

CHOOSING FRIENDS WISELY

*Do not be misled: "Bad company
corrupts good character."*
1 Corinthians 15:33 niv

Loving Savior, I know You want me to reach others for
You by living out my faith before them. But I also know
that I need to be wise in choosing the people I spend
my time with, because if I'm not careful, I could be led
into compromising situations. I need Your wisdom in
this part of my life. I need You to guide my steps as I
make my way through a world full of people who need
You but who would not make good, close friends for
me. Open my eyes to see who should be a good friend,
while helping me to avoid compromise.

EARTHLY AUTHORITY

Let everyone be subject to the governing authorities, for there is no authority except that which God has established. The authorities that exist have been established by God. Consequently, whoever rebels against the authority is rebelling against what God has instituted, and those who do so will bring judgment on themselves.

ROMANS 13:1–2 NIV

Lord of lords, thank You for placing people in positions of authority so they can keep order in the world. I know that You have appointed those rulers, even those with whom I disagree. Father, I know that You want me to live in obedience to earthly law, as long as doing so doesn't cause me to disobey You. Help me to know the difference between laws that attempt to get me to compromise and those that don't.

PARDON

*And I will cleanse them from all their
iniquity, whereby they have sinned against
me; and I will pardon all their iniquities,
whereby they have sinned, and whereby
they have transgressed against me.*

JEREMIAH 33:8 KJV

★ ★ ★

Father, there was a time when I had the nagging uncertainty about whether I had been truly forgiven. I had remorse for my sins, I repented of my actions, and I desired to understand the truth of the Gospel. But as a new Christian, I tried unsuccessfully to live up to the contradictory advice I was given. Today I know that I cannot earn a place in Your kingdom by what I do or avoid doing. Instead, I bring You a heart of obedience and an affection for spiritual matters. I am secure in the knowledge of Your saving grace. I honor You with a heart of obedience and know that when I fail, You will pardon me.

NOBLE CHARACTER

A wife of noble character who can find? She is worth far more than rubies. . . . Her children arise and call her blessed; her husband also, and he praises her: "Many women do noble things, but you surpass them all."

PROVERBS 31:10, 28–29 NIV

Blessed Father, my life is so busy, and sometimes I neglect the basics of family life, such as speaking uplifting, encouraging words to my wife. She is a blessing to me, so I want to make it a point not just to treat her with respect and love, but also to compliment her for who she is and what she does for me. Remind me to tell my wife every day how much I love her, value her, and appreciate everything she does for me, for our children, and for others.

PANIC

And he said unto me, My grace is sufficient for thee: for my strength is made perfect in weakness.

2 CORINTHIANS 12:9 KJV

★ ★ ★

Dear Lord, when evil unleashes its destructive forces, I feel overwhelmed. Whether it is an unexpected financial upheaval, a change in work assignment, an unfavorable doctor's report, or a personal crisis, panic bubbles below the surface. Dread hovers over me like an oppressive cloud and dampens my spirit. Fear and doubt create havoc in my otherwise rational mind. Because panic becomes contagious and sets off a frenzy around me, I must not give in to panic. I pray for You to silence the alarms in my life. Teach me to be composed in the midst of uncertainty.

CUTTING WORDS

Some people make cutting remarks,
but the words of the wise bring healing.
PROVERBS 12:18 NLT

Lord, sometimes it seems like my Christian brothers and I spend more time making cutting, sarcastic remarks to one another—remarks we don't really mean—than we do speaking words of healing and encouragement. My friends are important to me, and I know they are a blessing from You. Help me to be careful not to go too far when I'm teasing them, but even more than that, give me uplifting, encouraging, healing words to speak to them. And when I'm frustrated or angry with someone, help me to check my words so that I don't say anything that cuts down that person. Give me the wisdom to know what I should and should not say.

MAKING MISTAKES

*As far as the east is from the west, so far
hath he removed our transgressions from us.*
PSALM 103:12 KJV

★ ★ ★

Father, I am always making mistakes. As a child, I used an eraser to rub out the errors and correct them, although the erasures were obvious on the paper. More recently, I used touch-up paint to cover scratches on doorframes, although getting the paints to match exactly was impossible.

O Lord, I sometimes make bad judgments and sin against You. Within my own power, I cannot correct those mistakes, but I trust in Jesus to blot out all my iniquities. When You remove them, You don't leave a smudgy erasure or a mismatched touch-up. Thank You for removing them entirely, so they no longer exist.

GOD'S OWN WORDS

*All Scripture is God-breathed and is useful for
teaching, rebuking, correcting and training in
righteousness, so that the servant of God may
be thoroughly equipped for every good work.*
2 TIMOTHY 3:16–17 NIV

Father, thank You for speaking through the people
who wrote the scriptures. You use their words to help
me know You better and to provide me all I need to
be equipped to live a life that pleases You. I know I
should focus on all of the Bible, not just my favorite
passages or verses, for the whole Bible is Your communication with me. Your Word is trustworthy, and it
contains everything I need to know about You and
Your will for my life. Your Word is useful to me because
it prepares me to do what You have called me to do.

GOD RELIANCE

The LORD is nigh unto them that are of a broken heart; and saveth such as be of a contrite spirit.
PSALM 34:18 KJV

Dear Lord, when a friend sees my distress and offers his support, my tendency is to wave him away and assure him that nothing is required from him. I think I can take care of myself.

Father, I am also reluctant to pray about those burdens that I think I should be able to handle without Your help. Help me realize that no matter how independent I may wish to be, I must come to You with a humble and contrite heart. Forgive me for my attempts at self-sufficiency, and show me how to accept help from others and from You.

A TOOL FOR EVERY TASK

I therefore, the prisoner of the Lord,
beseech you that ye walk worthy of
the vocation wherewith ye are called.
EPHESIANS 4:1 KJV

Father, I am impressed when I watch a skilled carpenter or auto mechanic at work. I am struck by how they select a tool that is perfectly fitted for the task at hand. Dear Lord, I see that You have given me particular skills and abilities. Others can fill in for me when I do not do the jobs for which I have been created. However, You have called me into service to apply my unique talents to those tasks that I do best. May I never evade my responsibilities by claiming that someone else is better qualified.

CLOTHED IN RIGHTEOUSNESS

Because thou sayest, I am rich, and increased with goods, and have need of nothing; and knowest not that thou art wretched, and miserable, and poor, and blind, and naked.
REVELATION 3:17 KJV

Heavenly Father, although I do not think of myself as rich, I have always had a home, food, and clothing. I recognize my happy circumstances when I think of those prophets of old who had stones for their pillows. More important are the spiritual riches You give me. At one time I was walking in darkness, starved for love and unprotected from Satan. Now I am sheltered in Your love, nourished by Your Word, and clothed in the protection of the Holy Spirit. I love You, Lord, and will always be mindful of the rich blessings that fall on me.

RUNNING UNENCUMBERED

*Therefore, since we are surrounded by such
a great cloud of witnesses, let us throw off
everything that hinders and the sin that
so easily entangles. And let us run with
perseverance the race marked out for us,
fixing our eyes on Jesus, the pioneer
and perfecter of faith.*

HEBREWS 12:1–2 NIV

Father God, just as a distance runner wouldn't want to start his race carrying a heavy pack, I don't want anything hindering me as I run my race of faith. Lord, please reveal to me anything that could possibly slow me down or trip me up, and then give me the strength and perseverance it will take to finish strong. Above all, help me keep my focus on Jesus and Him alone. Thank You, Lord, for inviting me to take part in the race.

Day 36

GRACE

Wherefore we receiving a kingdom which cannot be moved, let us have grace, whereby we may serve God acceptably with reverence and godly fear.
HEBREWS 12:28 KJV

Father, I know that I cannot obtain absolute perfection in my life. I appeal to You for Your mercy. I know that Your forgiveness is without limit, provided I exercise the same forgiveness with others. I pray for the help of the Holy Spirit so I can forgive repeatedly without harboring resentment. Thank You for Your generous grace. I ask that Your mercy flow over me. I pray that You will favor my undertakings and wrap them in Your clemency so that even when I fail, I will be under Your protection.

★ CHRIST LIVING IN YOU ★

I have been crucified with Christ; it is no longer I who live, but Christ lives in me; and the life which I now live in the flesh I live by faith in the Son of God, who loved me and gave Himself for me.

GALATIANS 2:20 NKJV

Lord Jesus, I want to live like You lived, love like You loved, give like You gave, and forgive like You forgave when You were here on earth. I want to be an imitation of You in all these ways and more, but my own desires often get in the way. Help me to deny myself daily, to take up my cross and follow You. I can only do that by faith in You, so help me to so fully trust and believe You that my life looks more like Yours every day.

Day 38

WORTHY OF HONOR

*O LORD our Lord, how excellent
is thy name in all the earth!*
PSALM 8:9 KJV

O Lord, I have gazed through a telescope and seen stars and galaxies uncountable. I have peered into a microscope and seen a world in one drop of water. When I see the majesty of Your vast creation, I am brought to my knees in wonder. But in my humble admiration, there is also a desperate question: do You notice me and concern Yourself with me? I thank You, Lord, for personally answering my question. When I am apprehensive, I put my trust in You, and You keep me safe. When I am lonely, You talk to me. When I am sad, You make me happy. When I am weak, I bow before You and feel Your strength.

FOOLISH ARGUMENTS

*Don't have anything to do with foolish and
stupid arguments, because you know they
produce quarrels. And the Lord's servant
must not be quarrelsome but must be kind
to everyone, able to teach, not resentful.*

2 TIMOTHY 2:23–24 NIV

God of peace, many of us enjoy a good debate, and I know You want men to stand for Your true Gospel. Your written Word doesn't tell me to avoid controversies at all cost. You call me to contend for the faith, to stand against bad teaching, and to speak the truth in love. But I need Your wisdom as I do these things. Help me to know when to speak up and when to hold my tongue. And above all, help me to avoid useless arguments over things that aren't important. May I always speak gently and lovingly to those who need to hear Your truth.

CONFESSION

Whosoever shall confess that Jesus is the Son of God, God dwelleth in him, and he in God.

1 JOHN 4:15 KJV

★ ★ ★

Father, I confess that my life is not all that it should be. Even by my own standards, I fall far below what I want to accomplish. I can never be a perfect Christian, and my distress becomes even greater when I compare myself to Jesus. Dear Savior, my heart rejoices because my life becomes acceptable to You when I put on the cloak of Jesus. He brings me to all righteousness. I will confess my sins, renew myself in You, and set out again refreshed, determined to do better.

GOD'S PERFECT TIMING

The Lord isn't really being slow about his promise, as some people think. No, he is being patient for your sake. He does not want anyone to be destroyed, but wants everyone to repent.

2 PETER 3:9 NLT

Sovereign God, Your timing isn't like my timing. You exist and rule outside of any human time constraints, and You alone control the timing of all the events leading to Christ's return. I want Him to come back soon to set all things right and establish His eternal kingdom. But You, being the perfect example of love, wait—because You want to give all people a chance to turn to You. Help me to live my life here on earth as if Jesus won't return in my lifetime but also to work and live as if He's coming back today. Either way, You win—and so do I.

═══ **SECURE IN GOD'S LOVE** ═══

*"The LORD your God is with you, the Mighty
Warrior who saves. He will take great delight
in you; in his love he will no longer rebuke
you, but will rejoice over you with singing."*

ZEPHANIAH 3:17 NIV

Loving heavenly Father, so often I wonder how a holy
God like You can take any pleasure in a man like me.
I wonder how You can love me and take delight in
me—how You could possibly take such joy in me that
You would actually *sing* over me. But You not only
promise to save me and be with me always, You tell
me that You joy in me as Your own son. When I feel
insecure in my relationship with You, remind me that
You are tender and affectionate in Your fatherly love.

═ **COMPASSION AND FORGIVENESS** ═

*Be kind and compassionate to
one another, forgiving each other,
just as in Christ God forgave you.*
EPHESIANS 4:32 NIV

Loving Father, it was with great compassion and love
that You reached down to me and welcomed me into
Your heavenly kingdom. I didn't deserve it—You did it
because of who You are. You've told me that I am to
extend that same kind of compassion and forgiveness
to those who sin against me. I confess that it's not in
my nature to respond to others that way. I feel as if
I'm entitled to hang on to anger, especially against
those who hurt me intentionally. Lord, forgive me for
my lack of compassion and for my unforgiving heart.
Help me to forgive not because someone deserves it,
but because it's part of who I am in You.

YOUR SOURCE OF POWER

"This is the word of the LORD to Zerubbabel:
'Not by might nor by power, but by my
Spirit,' says the LORD Almighty."
ZECHARIAH 4:6 NIV

Almighty God, I confess that I have a big streak of self-reliance. Sometimes I feel like I can do what You've called me to do under my own power. But Jesus, You told Your followers that apart from You, we can do nothing. I know You can use my strengths and talents to accomplish big things for Your kingdom. But that can only happen when I bring all I am to You. Lord, I know You don't want to share Your glory with anybody, so help me to humble myself and come to You daily, knowing that I can't do anything without You.

HEARING AND DOING

*But don't just listen to God's word.
You must do what it says. Otherwise,
you are only fooling yourselves.*
JAMES 1:22 NLT

Lord my God, I confess that I don't always act on what I read in Your written Word. Sometimes, I see some great truth but then go about my day as if I have no idea what I've read. Please forgive me. I know You want me to read from the Bible every day, but I also know it's even more important that I act on what I've read. Your written Word is filled cover-to-cover with wisdom and commands. But they won't mean a thing to me unless I obey. Through Your Spirit, make the Word come alive to me so that I can do what it says.

OVERCOMING FEAR

Watch ye, stand fast in the faith,
quit you like men, be strong.
1 CORINTHIANS 16:13 KJV

★ ★ ★

Father, I pray that I can overcome fears that hinder me from following in Your footsteps. Fear makes me a liar: I excuse myself by claiming that I don't know how or that I'm not ready. Fear makes me a pretender: I can be fainthearted or hesitant, and I call it patience.

Regardless of the nature of my anxiety, I must press ahead. Lord, may I embrace Your Word in order to drive out irrational concerns that trouble my heart. I pray that I will not allow fear to paralyze me.

★ LEADING BY SERVING ★

*But Jesus called them to Himself and said,
"You know that the rulers of the Gentiles lord
it over them, and those who are great exercise
authority over them. Yet it shall not be so
among you; but whoever desires to become
great among you, let him be your servant."*

MATTHEW 20:25–26 NKJV

Lord of my life, the world's picture of a great leader is far different from Yours. Most people believe that a great leader should be a strong man who knows how to exercise his authority over others. You, however, told Your followers that a great leader is one who makes *serving others* his priority. I believe You've called me to lead others in some capacity. Help me always to remember that Your kind of leader is one who serves first.

BEYOND THE MUNDANE

Therefore, my beloved brethren, be ye
stedfast, unmoveable, always abounding
in the work of the Lord, forasmuch as ye
know that your labour is not in vain in the Lord.
1 Corinthians 15:58 KJV

Dear Father, contentment and satisfaction are a small step apart. I pray that I will never be too satisfied with myself or become too comfortable in my situation. May my contentment be one of action instead of ease. Lord, I ask You to show me the doors of opportunity that I can open to grow and improve. Should I refuse to open those doors, then jar me out of my routine and force me out of my comfort zone. If I do exactly the same thing each day in exactly the same way, then I should not expect results any different from the day before. Help me push beyond the mundane into the realm of active service.

THE SIMPLICITY OF SERVING GOD

O people, the LORD has told you what is good, and this is what he requires of you: to do what is right, to love mercy, and to walk humbly with your God.

MICAH 6:8 NLT

Heavenly Father, thank You for making things simple for me. I confess that I tend to make serving and loving You more complicated than You have. It seems like human beings can't just take You at Your Word—simply loving You and humbly walking with You in the way You've wanted us to since the very beginning. When I love You from my heart, the good You want me to do for You and others will flow from within me—it won't be a burden. Life is often difficult and complicated. I thank You that my walk with You doesn't have to be.

Day 50

ILLUMINATE BUT DON'T BLIND

Ye are all the children of light, and the children of the day: we are not of the night, nor of darkness.

1 THESSALONIANS 5:5 KJV

Lord, the other night during a power failure, I was the first to find a flashlight. The little light was enough to dispel the darkness. Because I carried the light, my family members gathered around me.

Your radiance illuminates all creation, yet I see people stumbling in spiritual gloom. Although I am but a pale reflection of Your brilliance, I pray that my teaching will become a beacon that draws lost souls into the circle of Your light. May my light never dazzle but rather reveal. Guide me so that I push out the darkness and fill others' lives with the light of Christ.

GRACIOUS GIFT

*For all things are for your sakes, that the abundant
grace might through the thanksgiving of
many redound to the glory of God.*

2 CORINTHIANS 4:15 KJV

Father, I express to You my thanksgiving for all that
You provide. I know that all good things come from
You. It is not by my hands or my ability but by Your
gracious gifts that I am able to earn a living and provide
for my family.

Dear Provider, as I employ the skills You have
given me to accomplish my duties in the workday world,
so I pray that I will employ my talents in the spiritual
world. I pray that I will use my talents to show Your
love to others.

STAYING STRONG

"Yet now be strong, Zerubbabel," says the LORD;
"and be strong, Joshua, son of Jehozadak,
the high priest; and be strong, all you people
of the land," says the LORD, "and work;
for I am with you," says the LORD of hosts.

HAGGAI 2:4 NKJV

★ ★ ★

Father, I thank You for always being there for me. I praise You for the wisdom to know when I need Your help and encouragement as I work to accomplish a task You've given me to do. I confess that I don't always turn to You first when the going is tough. Sometimes, I turn to others for strength and encouragement. But even though You've placed fellow believers in my life so we can strengthen and encourage one other, You want me to make Your presence my first source of everything I need to get the job done.

GOD'S WILL FOR YOU

Rejoice always; pray without ceasing;
in everything give thanks; for this is
God's will for you in Christ Jesus.
1 Thessalonians 5:16–18 NASB

Father in heaven, thank You for giving us clear instructions on Your will in 1 Thessalonians 5. But I confess that rejoicing always, praying without ceasing, and giving thanks in everything don't come easily to me. In fact, there are times when I don't feel like doing *any* of these things. You don't call me to live by my feelings, though, but by faith in You. That, Lord, is Your will for me. So help me to focus not on my circumstances but on You and Your blessings to me. Remind me often how important it is that I consistently come to You in prayer.

AN ETERNAL INHERITANCE

I will open my mouth with a parable; I will utter hidden things, things from of old—things we have heard and known, things our ancestors have told us. We will not hide them from their descendants; we will tell the next generation the praiseworthy deeds of the LORD, his power, and the wonders he has done.

PSALM 78:2–4 NIV

Father in heaven, I want to work hard and manage my assets wisely so I can leave my kids some kind of inheritance. But more than that, I want to leave them an inheritance that lasts into their own eternity, by instilling in them a love for You. Strengthen and encourage me to do that by reminding me of the tangible ways You've already blessed me. Lord, show me how I can leave behind a legacy of godliness and love for Your Word.

ENTER WITH THANKSGIVING

*And God said unto Moses, I Am That I Am:
and he said, Thus shalt thou say unto the
children of Israel, I Am hath sent me unto you.*

EXODUS 3:14 KJV

Father, I pray that I may always enter Your presence in the proper way. I resolve to acknowledge with thanksgiving what You have done for me. You are merciful, long-suffering, and mindful of me. I praise You for the blessings that flow from You.

Lord, I come before You with humility. I bow before You, the Creator who called everything into existence. I bow in awe of You as I realize You are the I AM, the eternal presence that has spanned the ages. I humbly cry to You as my provider and deliverer.

Day 56

"LITTLE" SINS?

*But now is the time to get rid of anger, rage,
malicious behavior, slander, and dirty language.*
Colossians 3:8 NLT

★ ★ ★

Father in heaven, I confess that I sometimes think of
behaviors such as fits of anger, talking about others
in a negative way, and profanity as "little sins"—as if
they're not as bad in Your eyes as murder or adultery.
Help me to change my thinking about the sins listed
in Colossians 3:8, and then help me to change my behavior. Instead of being easily angered, I want to be a
patient person who repays evil with good. Instead of
being a gossip, I want to be a man who only speaks well
of others. And instead of speaking profanities, I want
to be someone whose language always glorifies You.

GOD'S PLANS FOR YOU

"For I know the plans I have for you," declares the LORD, "plans to prosper you and not to harm you, plans to give you hope and a future."
JEREMIAH 29:11 NIV

★ ★ ★

Loving Father, many men love to make plans. We plan for our families, for our professional pursuits, and even for our spiritual ministries. As I make my plans, though, help me to remember that You already have my future mapped out. Give me an ear to hear what You've said about Your plans for me, and a pliable heart and mind so that I can adjust my plans to align with Yours. Give me the inner peace that comes from knowing that You love me and that You will never steer me wrong.

LONG–HAUL ENDURANCE

*For the which cause I also suffer these things:
nevertheless I am not ashamed: for I know
whom I have believed, and am persuaded
that he is able to keep that which I have
committed unto him against that day.*

2 TIMOTHY 1:12 KJV

Lord, when my duties and obligations become too much for me, I ask why I must endure them. Yet, I read Your Word and understand that when I am beaten down, I am not defeated. Minor problems are opportunities for growth and prepare me for the major crises I will surely face along the way. You are equipping me to succeed despite momentary setbacks. Prepare me to endure, not for a moment but for a lifetime. Teach me to develop the stamina to overcome not only momentary challenges but also trials that may last a lifetime.

CONFESSION TO YOUR BROTHERS

Confess your sins to each other and pray for each other so that you may be healed. The earnest prayer of a righteous person has great power and produces wonderful results.

JAMES 5:16 NLT

Father in heaven, I confess that, like most men, I am not usually comfortable sharing my struggles and failures with others. I don't like making myself vulnerable, and I worry that my brothers in the faith would look down on me if they knew about my hidden sins. But You, in Your wisdom, tell me I should confess my sins to others so that they can pray for me and hold me accountable. Humble me, and help me to understand how important it is that I make myself accountable to my brothers in the faith.

Day 60

SPIRITUAL TRAINING

For physical training is of some value, but godliness has value for all things, holding promise for both the present life and the life to come. This is a trustworthy saying that deserves full acceptance.

1 TIMOTHY 4:8–9 NIV

★ ★ ★

Father in heaven, thank You for giving me my physical body. I know You want me to take care of it so that I can live a healthy life and serve You better. Help me to focus not just on my physical health but on my spiritual health as well. As I care for my inner man so that I can be more and more godly every day, show me what is beneficial to read, view, listen to, and talk about. Turn my attention toward those things, and away from the things that bring me down. Above all, never let me neglect spending time in Your presence.

WHEN YOU SIN

My dear children, I am writing this to you so that
you will not sin. But if anyone does sin, we have
an advocate who pleads our case before the Father.
He is Jesus Christ, the one who is truly righteous.
He himself is the sacrifice that atones for our sins—
and not only our sins but the sins of all the world.

1 JOHN 2:1–2 NLT

God of grace and forgiveness, thank You for sending Jesus, Your only Son, to earth so that I can be forgiven for my sins. You have transformed my thinking and behavior, but I still do things I know don't please or glorify You. Thank You, Jesus, for pleading my case before the Father. Thank You for making me righteous in Your eyes, even after I blow it. And when I do sin, may I confess it and turn away from it quickly.

GROWING STRONGER
THROUGH SUFFERING

*Not only so, but we also glory in our sufferings,
because we know that suffering produces
perseverance; perseverance, character; and character,
hope. And hope does not put us to shame, because
God's love has been poured out into our hearts
through the Holy Spirit, who has been given to us.*
ROMANS 5:3–5 NIV

Father in heaven, I confess that when I'm going through difficulties, my mind doesn't automatically go to the good You can grow in me as I endure. But Your Word promises that I can take heart when I'm suffering because my own difficulties help me to develop a stronger, more consistent faith. While You never called me to enjoy life's difficulties, You have told me that I can rejoice in them—for they can increase my faith and draw me closer to You.

GOD'S SPIRIT WITHIN YOU

"I will ask the Father, and he will give you another Advocate, who will never leave you. He is the Holy Spirit, who leads into all truth. The world cannot receive him, because it isn't looking for him and doesn't recognize him. But you know him, because he lives with you now and later will be in you."

JOHN 14:16–17 NLT

Lord Jesus, before Your death on the Cross, You promised Your followers that God's own Spirit would reside within them as they undertook their mission to do what was humanly impossible. I need Your Spirit today and every day. Thank You that in any struggle I face, be it spiritual, emotional, or physical, I can rely on Your Holy Spirit to guide me, to give me wisdom, and to strengthen me. Without Him, I'm weak and powerless. But with Him, I can do anything and everything You've asked of me.

Day 64

═══ **TRUE FRIENDSHIP** ═══

Better is open rebuke than hidden love.
Wounds from a friend can be trusted,
but an enemy multiplies kisses.
PROVERBS 27:5–6 NIV

Father in heaven, You've given me some good friends, and I'm grateful for that. I'm especially close to a few of those men, so close that we're able to challenge one another, encourage one another, and even rebuke one another when needed. It's not easy to speak tough truths to anyone, even those I'm closest to, and it's harder still when my friends speak those tough truths to me. But I need that kind of friend. I need men in my life who care enough to speak honestly when they see I'm going off track. Thank You for those friends. Help me to *be* that kind of friend.

TELL THE TRUTH

*Do not lie to each other, since you have
taken off your old self with its practices.*
COLOSSIANS 3:9 NIV

★ ★ ★

God of all truth, I'm so often faced with situations
where it seems advantageous to speak half-truths,
white lies, or outright lies—even to my own family or
my brothers and sisters in Christ. Help me to overcome the temptation to be anything less than honest,
especially when telling the truth hurts. Lord, I know
that You hate lies and that I will face consequences
when I willfully speak untruths. But I also know that
I glorify You and preserve my earthly relationships
when I speak only the truth. I want to glorify You in
everything I do and in everything I say, so guard my
heart and mouth from lies.

⚊ LOVING THE UNLOVING ⚊

*"But love your enemies, do good to them, and lend
to them without expecting to get anything back.
Then your reward will be great, and you will
be children of the Most High, because he is
kind to the ungrateful and wicked."*

LUKE 6:35 NIV

Lord Jesus, You set the perfect example of loving those
who hated You and of giving everything to those who,
like me, had nothing to give in return. I confess that I
struggle with loving those who don't love me in return,
and with doing good for them. But You never commanded Your followers to do something You weren't
willing to do Yourself. So You always empower us to
do as You have said. Help me to be kind and loving to
those who show no kindness in return. When I do that,
I'll be doing just like You did when You came to earth.

★ KEEPING THE PEACE ★

Never pay back evil for evil to anyone. Respect what is right in the sight of all men. If possible, so far as it depends on you, be at peace with all men. Never take your own revenge, beloved, but leave room for the wrath of God, for it is written, "Vengeance is Mine, I will repay," says the Lord.

ROMANS 12:17–19 NASB

God of peace, I live among people who are as fallen and sinful as I am. That means they often do things that hurt or anger me—sometimes accidentally and sometimes on purpose. That fallen, sinful side of me wants to strike back at people who do me wrong. But I know that You call the redeemed, transformed side of me to forgive those who sin against me. Give me a gracious, forgiving heart so that I can overcome the temptation to seek vengeance.

RESTORING A BROTHER

Brothers and sisters, if someone is caught in a sin, you who live by the Spirit should restore that person gently. But watch yourselves, or you also may be tempted. Carry each other's burdens, and in this way you will fulfill the law of Christ.

GALATIANS 6:1–2 NIV

★ ★ ★

God of forgiveness, I'm not always comfortable speaking words of correction, even when I know my brother in the faith needs to hear them. Give me the courage I need to speak up when necessary, and the wisdom to choose my words carefully. I don't want to come off as condemning, so give me a gentle spirit to speak words of encouragement and restoration when my brother has gone off course. Help me never to forget that if I'm not careful, I can stray off course myself.

A LIFE OF INTEGRITY

*Whoever walks in integrity walks securely,
but whoever takes crooked paths will be found out.*
PROVERBS 10:9 NIV

Lord Jesus, during Your time here on earth You were the perfect example of integrity. You never compromised when it came to following Your Father's law, and You never wavered in doing what He had sent You to do. Make me more like You every day. You made me a new creation when You brought me into Your family, and I want You and the rest of the family to see me as a man of integrity. Help me to be someone who follows Your Word first and who never compromises on what You tell me is right. Help me to love and obey You with a pure heart and with an eye toward Your eternal kingdom.

PEOPLE PLEASING?

Am I now trying to win the approval of human beings, or of God? Or am I trying to please people? If I were still trying to please people, I would not be a servant of Christ.

GALATIANS 1:10 NIV

Faithful God, I know that I can glorify You as I try to please certain other people—my wife, my boss, and those in authority over me. But I confess that I sometimes find myself trying to please other people with speech and behavior that doesn't please You. When I hear others speaking in ways I know aren't right, it's easy to join in to fit in. Father, forgive me for my lack of faithfulness to You and Your Word. Give me a heart and mind that are focused on pleasing You, not other men, first.

★ A PROPER SELF-IMAGE ★

For I say, through the grace given to me, to everyone who is among you, not to think of himself more highly than he ought to think, but to think soberly, as God has dealt to each one a measure of faith.

ROMANS 12:3 NKJV

Lord, it's often tempting to think more highly of myself than You would have me think. You don't call me to think self-abasing thoughts but to think of myself as simply a sinner who is saved through Your Son's work on the cross. In light of that, help me to remember that any good in me is on account of You and You alone. Thank You for Your love and for bringing me into Your eternal kingdom. May I always remember that the glory for doing that isn't on account of me.

SEEKING HELP

"You will surely wear out, both yourself and these people who are with you, for the task is too heavy for you; you cannot do it alone."

EXODUS 18:18 NASB

Father God, I sometimes feel overwhelmed when I think about the responsibilities You've given me. I want to serve You faithfully, I want to give my wife and children my very best, and I want to do my job in a way that pleases my employer and glorifies You. And that's just the very beginning of all You've given me to do. I sometimes feel like I need help, but I'm often reluctant to seek it out. Give me the wisdom and humility I need to reach out for help—both from my brothers here on earth and from You.

EQUIPPED TO DO GOD'S WILL

*Now may the God of peace who brought
up our Lord Jesus from the dead, that great
Shepherd of the sheep, through the blood of
the everlasting covenant, make you complete
in every good work to do His will, working in you
what is well pleasing in His sight, through Jesus
Christ, to whom be glory forever and ever. Amen.*

HEBREWS 13:20–21 NKJV

God of peace, thank You for sending Your Son to die
for my sins. In Your awesome power, You raised Him
from the dead and brought Him back to heaven to sit
at Your right hand. Thank You for showing me Your
will and for giving me good works to do here on earth.
Thank You too, for equipping me and preparing me
with all I need to faithfully and effectively serve You.
Remind me daily to seek out Your power and strength

GODLY EMPATHY

Rejoice with those who rejoice;
mourn with those who mourn.
ROMANS 12:15 NIV

God of compassion and comfort, You always know what is going on inside me. You know when I feel stressed or grieved, happy or sad. You know when I feel like just hiding away by myself, and You know when I'm at my sociable best. You know those things because You love me so personally. Thank You for loving me like that. Lord, help me to extend that kind of love to the people You've placed in my life. Give me a compassionate, empathetic heart, and make me sensitive to the needs of those around me. Help me to offer comfort to those who are grieving, words of encouragement for those who are enduring difficult times, and words of wisdom for those who aren't sure what to do. Finally, allow me the privilege of celebrating with those who are rejoicing.

COMFORT OF THE HOLY SPIRIT

But the Comforter. . .shall teach you all things,
and bring all things to your remembrance,
whatsoever I have said unto you.
JOHN 14:26 KJV

★ ★ ★

Lord Jesus, just before You ascended into heaven, the disciples wondered what would happen to them after You went away. You told them that You would send the Holy Spirit to be their comforter and teacher. By Your power they were able to boldly spread the Good News throughout the sinful world.

Today, Lord, I want to thank You for the gift of the Spirit working through Your children. I trust Your power to give me joy and hope. Produce spiritual fruit in my life and pour Your love in my heart by the Holy Spirit.

SEXUAL PURITY

For this is the will of God, your sanctification;
that is, that you abstain from sexual immorality;
that each of you know how to possess his own
vessel in sanctification and honor.

1 THESSALONIANS 4:3–4 NASB

Gracious heavenly Father, You didn't save me and bring me into Your eternal kingdom so that I could just go my own way and do whatever feels good. Every day, the world I live in fires all kinds of sexual temptations my way, and sometimes I feel almost overwhelmed. When I am tempted sexually, remind me that my body belongs to You—and that I am to honor You in everything I do. Help me to control my mind and my eyes first so that I can say "yes" to intimacy with You and "no" to intimacy with anyone who is not my wife.

HEAVENLY ROAD MAP

Come unto me, all ye that labour and are
heavy laden, and I will give you rest.
MATTHEW 11:28 KJV

Lord, I plan a driving trip in exhaustive detail, highlighting the best route on the map, pinning down stopovers, and identifying points of interest. All of this requires a great deal of study that begins weeks before the departure date.

Father, I pray that I might take far more care in planning my trip to heaven. I don't know how much time I have to prepare for it, but while there is still time, I will talk to You in prayer, study the Bible to learn Your will, and work to be a faithful servant. Write on my heart the heavenly road map.

★ BECAUSE OF HIS MERCY ★

He saved us, not because of righteous
things we had done, but because of his
mercy. He saved us through the washing
of rebirth and renewal by the Holy Spirit.

TITUS 3:5 NIV

Precious Savior, thank You for bringing me into Your eternal kingdom. You transformed me through the power of Your love and Your Holy Spirit. I know that You want me to do good works for Your kingdom and for other people. But those things happen *because* You've saved me, not so that I *can* be saved. There is nothing I do on my own to earn salvation from the consequences of my own sin. You've done it all, and because of that I've been reborn and renewed by Your Holy Spirit. Humble me and help me to focus on the fact that I'm saved only because of Your mercy.

IT'S NOT FAIR!

*In this meaningless life of mine I
have seen both of these: the righteous
perishing in their righteousness, and the
wicked living long in their wickedness.*
ECCLESIASTES 7:15 NIV

Righteous God, I just can't figure out why bad things
happen to good men while those who live unrighteous
lives prosper from their misdeeds. To me, it seems right
that a man who faithfully follows You would live a long,
prosperous life. But it doesn't always turn out that way.
Lord, in my limited human thinking, this seems unfair.
But I know You have reasons for doing what You do. I
don't ask for complete understanding of these things—
I just ask that You would help me to trust Your perfect judgment and timing. Remind me that, in the
end, You will set everything right.

Day 80

LOVE IN ACTION

*Dear children, let us not love with words
or speech but with actions and in truth.*

1 JOHN 3:18 NIV

My loving Father, sometimes it's easy for me to speak kind, loving words but difficult to put my love for You and for others into action. Forgive me when I fail to produce acts of love and kindness, and help me to love not just with my words but with my deeds. It's not always easy for a man to speak kind words, but it's sometimes even more difficult to love through what we do. So please provide me with opportunities to truly love others in ways that help them and glorify You. I thank You for Your love for me, and I ask You to help me to spread that love to other people with a heart of pure love.

STAND UP, SPEAK UP

*Speak up for those who cannot speak
for themselves, for the rights
of all who are destitute.*
PROVERBS 31:8 NIV

Compassionate God, I know there are any number of people groups who need someone to stand up and speak out on their behalf. I think of those who live in domestic and sexual slavery around the world. I think of the hungry, the homeless, and the infirm who live in my own community. It's sad to consider what so many unfortunate people have to endure in today's world. But I know that You love them and value them as much as You love and value me. So help me to be a voice for those who can't speak up for themselves.

═══ A FRIEND OF GOD ═══

And the scripture was fulfilled that says, "Abraham believed God, and it was credited to him as righteousness," and he was called God's friend.
JAMES 2:23 NIV

Lord, I've never had a problem with thinking of You as the Creator, and I've come to a place where I think of You as a loving heavenly Father. But my friend? That one stops me every time. Your Word talks about the men You called Your friends, and most important of all, Your Son Jesus said of His followers, "I have called you friends, for everything that I learned from my Father I have made known to you." Father, I believe You always keep Your promises, and that makes me Your friend. And You aren't just any friend but my best friend.

HANDLING TEMPTATION

No temptation has overtaken you except such as is common to man; but God is faithful, who will not allow you to be tempted beyond what you are able, but with the temptation will also make the way of escape, that you may be able to bear it.

1 CORINTHIANS 10:13 NKJV

Lord Jesus, I know that all men are tempted in one way or another. Satan tempted You at the start of Your earthly ministry, but You never sinned. I believe You beat temptation that day because You knew how to handle it. You relied on Your heavenly Father and on His Word. Lord, keep me humble—may I never believe that I have the ability to overcome temptation without Your help. Remind me to call out to You, and show me how I can best fight temptation.

UPRIGHTNESS

So the king gave the order, and they brought Daniel and threw him into the lions' den. The king said to Daniel, "May your God, whom you serve continually, rescue you!"

DANIEL 6:10 NIV

★ ★ ★

Lord, I want to live an upright life no matter how difficult the circumstances. I look to Daniel as an example of one who was not afraid to do what was right, even though he faced death in a den of lions. You gave him protection and blessed his integrity.

When I face tough times, I pray I will continue to put my trust in You, O Lord. Give me a strong faith like Daniel's. You are more powerful than any enemies of my soul, and You have every situation in my life under control.

═ ★ REVIVE ME ★ ═

Nevertheless I have somewhat against
thee, because thou hast left thy first love.
Remember therefore from whence thou art
fallen, and repent, and do the first works.
REVELATION 2:4–5 KJV

Father, I sometimes become so captivated by the concerns of my daily life that I lose interest in my spiritual life. I struggle through a morass of unconcern for others and even for myself. I forget my calling as Your child.

Lord, I acknowledge my apathy and ignorance and realize that my lassitude comes from a lack of drinking from Your refreshing water. I need to renew myself with prayer, study of Your Word, and fellowship with other Christians. Give me new momentum. Revitalize my life. Restore the intensity of my first love for You.

A SPIRIT OF COURAGE

*For God hath not given us the spirit of fear;
but of power, and of love, and of a sound mind.*
2 TIMOTHY 1:7 KJV

Father, fear and anxiety are twin thieves that rob me of my tranquility. I can't sleep, I can't eat, and I can't think. Fear saps my strength, muddles my mind, and weakens my spirit. Fear is always there, lurking in the shadows, ready to snatch away my willingness to confront challenges. Lord, I pray that courage would dominate my fears so that I may be undaunted and uncowed. Prayer and study of Your Word will build my courage because knowledge and love overcome fear. Grant me confidence and a clear head when it is time for me to choose between courage and fear, truth and lies, right and wrong.

LOVE

*Know therefore that the L ORD thy God, he is
God, the faithful God, which keepeth covenant
and mercy with them that love him and keep his
commandments to a thousand generations.*
D EUTERONOMY 7:9 KJV

Omnipotent Father, there are no limitations to the
amount of love and attention You can bestow upon
each of Your children. Although I receive Your rich
blessings all the time, day and night, I pray that I will
not take Your love for granted.

Lord, the more I know You and understand You, the
more I will see and appreciate Your love. I pray that I
will experience You more deeply so that my love for
You will increase. You have taught me that sacrifices
must be made for love to grow. I submit to You. Demol-
ish me and then rebuild me so I may be one with You.

TRUSTING GOD
WITH THE BAD STUFF

*And we know that God causes all things to work
together for good to those who love God, to those
who are called according to His purpose.*

Romans 8:28 nasb

Lord, You know that not everything that happens to me is good. Getting sick is not good. Neither is losing my job. And getting into a serious auto accident can throw a man's life into turmoil. But good can come out of any of those things—and many others—because I know You and am committed to following You through even the worst of circumstances. You've promised that You make all things work together for my good, making a positive out of things that are clearly negative. Please give me the faith and the peace to wait on You to do that.

═══ EQUAL IN HONOR ═══

Honour all men. Love the brotherhood.
Fear God. Honour the king.
1 PETER 2:17 KJV

Father, You have made me a unique individual. You have bestowed upon me a unique dignity. I may gain wealth or descend into poverty, become well-known or live in obscurity, receive prestige or be ignored. Regardless of those circumstances, I am equal in honor with everyone else because I am made in Your image.

Remind me, O Lord, that the truth of equal honor applies to others I meet. May I treat them with dignity and respect and see Your likeness in them.

EMERGENCY RESPONSE

The LORD is my shepherd; I shall not want. He maketh me to lie down in green pastures: he leadeth me beside the still waters. He restoreth my soul.

PSALM 23:1–3 KJV

Father, the feeling of foreboding was upon me again. I knew that something awful was going to happen. So I came to You in prayer and read the Psalms. That time of meditation cleared the mental overcast. I saw that the day was bright and sunny, and the disasters I had imagined never occurred.

Father, help me keep the well of anxiety empty. Prevent me from refilling it by brooding over past events or imagining future disasters. Help me face the issues that cause my anxiety and build my response upon realistic assumptions. I will stay in touch with You so that I may look to the future with hope.

IN HIS TIMING

"God is not a man, that He should lie,
nor a son of man, that He should repent;
has He said, and will He not do it? Or has
He spoken, and will He not make it good?"

NUMBERS 23:19 NASB

Trustworthy God, I've known people who I couldn't trust to keep their word. They may have made promises with the best of intentions, but they didn't always live up to their vows. It's never that way with You—never! You keep every one of Your promises and fulfill all Your purposes. I can trust You, even when Your timing differs from what I would want. But You are far wiser than I am, and I have to trust that You will fulfill Your promises when Your timing is right.

★ A GIFT FROM GOD ★

Give, and it shall be given unto you. . . .
For with the same measure that ye mete
withal it shall be measured to you again.
LUKE 6:38 KJV

Lord, You set the standard for generosity by giving up Your life for a sinful world. May I always be reminded of Your sacrifice when I see a need that I can fill. Just as a farmer plants seeds and profits from the harvest, You also bless those who share their assets.

Heavenly Father, help me to give out of a pure motive to bless those in need, not out of a selfish expectation of reward. I truly want to act as Your hand extended to help those who have physical, spiritual, and financial needs.

FORGIVEN!

How blessed is he whose transgression is forgiven,
whose sin is covered! How blessed is the man
to whom the Lord does not impute iniquity,
and in whose spirit there is no deceit!

PSALM 32:1–2 NASB

God of forgiveness, I cannot thank You enough for forgiving my sins when I come to You in confession. You have assured me that when I confess my wrong-doing, You are faithful and just to completely forgive me and completely cleanse me. When You forgive my sins, You also choose to put them out of Your mind, casting them into a deep sea of divine forgetfulness. Lord, when I sin, move me to confess it quickly and turn away from it so that I can be clean before You.

HERE I STAND

*"Whoever believes in me, as Scripture has said,
rivers of living water will flow from within them."*
JOHN 7:38 NIV

★ ★ ★

Lord Jesus, thank You for Your promise of life flowing from within me because I know and follow You. Thank You for dying for my sin and thank You for infusing me, through the power of Your Holy Spirit, with the boldness I need to proclaim Your truth in a world that often doesn't want to hear it. Whether I'm sharing Your message with an eager audience or trying to speak it in an unfriendly environment, give me strength and wisdom so that I don't shrink away from what You've called me to do.

FOCUSING ON THE ETERNAL

We do not look at the things which are seen, but at the things which are not seen. For the things which are seen are temporary, but the things which are not seen are eternal.

2 CORINTHIANS 4:18 NKJV

Eternal God, Your written Word gives me many clues as to what waits for me in eternity. Some of what I can see in the natural realm, the things here on earth, are pleasant and wonderful to view. Others aren't so pleasant—there is a lot of ugliness in this world, and many people suffer because of it. But the beauty I can see here is nothing compared with what I'll witness in heaven. And the ugliness will be a distant memory once I'm in Your eternal kingdom. May I keep my focus on the eternal, not on what is here on earth.

GREET THEM WITH A SMILE

But straightway Jesus spake unto them, saying,
Be of good cheer; it is I; be not afraid.
MATTHEW 14:27 KJV

Dear Jesus, just as You told Your followers to be of good cheer, may I recognize that You want me to heed those words as well. My experience confirms what scientific research has shown—a cheerful personality can overcome physical and mental afflictions. A positive attitude allows the body to heal.

Lord, give me a cheerful disposition, not only to benefit myself but also to bless others. I know that a good attitude can be a great influence for You. Help my joy spread to all those I meet.

═ PLANTING THE RIGHT SEEDS ═

*Do not be deceived: God cannot be mocked.
A man reaps what he sows. Whoever sows to
please their flesh, from the flesh will reap
destruction; whoever sows to please the Spirit,
from the Spirit will reap eternal life.*

GALATIANS 6:7–8 NIV

★ ★ ★

Righteous God, You've arranged life on this earth so that a man's thoughts and actions have consequences. I know that if I live and think according to Your will, I'll see good results. . .and if I don't, I won't. Lord, I want to reap the harvest of eternal life—not just for myself but also for those You've placed in my life. Keep me mindful of the importance of living the way You've called me to live, and not in a way that pleases my own desires.

FIRST THINGS FIRST

*But seek ye first the kingdom of God,
and his righteousness; and all these
things shall be added unto you.*

MATTHEW 6:33 KJV

Lord, each day I rush around to finish a multitude of minor tasks that absolutely, positively have to be done by the evening deadline. I am assailed from all sides as if swimming with a school of piranhas. Each one nibbles away at my time. Each task by itself would be a minor distraction, but together, they crowd out important duties.

From Your wisdom, Lord, I want to understand what matters most. Bring order to the chaos of my daily life. Help me identify the proper priorities and organize my life around them.

WHERE TO TURN
WHEN TIMES ARE TOUGH

The LORD is good, a refuge in times of trouble.
He cares for those who trust in him.

NAHUM 1:7 NIV

Lord Jesus, when I first came to know You, I thought the rest of my life would be easy. It wasn't long, though, before I found out that walking with You presented its own difficulties. You didn't let me waver, and over time You've taught me the importance of turning to You when I face problems. Thank You for loving me and for always being my refuge. Help me to trust You for protection and empowerment when I'm going through rough times.

Day 100

HEAVENLY COMPASS

And the very God of peace sanctify you wholly;
and I pray God your whole spirit and soul
and body be preserved blameless unto
the coming of our Lord Jesus Christ.

1 THESSALONIANS 5:23 KJV

Dear Lord, when I am hiking with my children, I am constantly checking my direction with a compass and a trail guide. The little ones depend on me to set the right course for them. As a compass is drawn to the north, so I am drawn to You, knowing that others follow in my steps.

Heavenly Father, my soul seeks to align with Your mercy and grace. You, O Lord, are my righteous Creator. I pray that I will live a consecrated life through Your enabling power. Please guide me to live right and dispel the negative powers that could draw me off course.

SEEING GOD'S
CREATIVITY IN NATURE

"But ask the animals, and they will teach you, or the birds in the sky, and they will tell you; or speak to the earth, and it will teach you, or let the fish in the sea inform you. Which of all these does not know that the hand of the LORD has done this?"

JOB 12:7–9 NIV

Creator God, thank You for making such a beautiful universe, including the planet I live on. I enjoy seeing everything from a magnificent mountain range to a tiny hummingbird feeding from a flower. Lord, I don't literally see You when I'm hiking a nature trail, fishing at a free-flowing stream, climbing a mountain, or going birdwatching. But I can see something of Your character and Your creativity, and that makes the time I spend enjoying nature all the more special.

VITAL GIVING

The thoughts of the diligent tend
only to plenteousness; but of every
one that is hasty only to want.
PROVERBS 21:5 KJV

Lord, it seems every cause has a compelling reason for me to support its effort. I find it difficult to separate the vital few from the trivial many. I cannot learn enough about every group's programs to fully support what they are doing. Give me the wisdom to direct my support to those who are carrying out Your will. I pray I will always be willing to make sacrifices, but keep me from being a wasteful giver.

Heavenly Father, guide me to practical ways that I can support those who are doing Your will.

★ SINFUL ANGER ★

"In your anger do not sin": Do not let the
sun go down while you are still angry,
and do not give the devil a foothold.
Ephesians 4:26–27 niv

Righteous Father, nowhere does Your Word tell me that anger is sinful in and of itself. In fact, it tells me that even You sometimes feel righteous anger. Sometimes I get angry over the same things that anger You, but I also feel anger over what I consider personal insults or slights. Whatever the cause, please help me to handle my anger in ways that don't lead me to sin. When I'm angry over injustice or unrighteousness, help me not to cross the line and start hating the perpetrators. And when I'm angry for personal reasons, keep me from lashing out in any way. Instead, help me to quickly reconcile and make peace with those who have angered me.

DESTRUCTIVE DEPENDENCIES

A good man sheweth favour, and lendeth:
he will guide his affairs with discretion.
PSALM 112:5 KJV

Heavenly Father, I see destructive dependencies creeping up on me. An innocuous hobby may become an all-consuming interest. Other dependencies are clearly harmful: those of a sexual nature or addictions to narcotics, alcohol, or gambling. They follow a distressing progression: At first I am repelled by them; slowly I begin to tolerate them; then I secretly participate in them; finally I actively promote them. I become a shell of a person, a ghost ship without a helmsman. The dependencies cause damage not only to me but also to those I love. Lord, I understand that habits can be good or bad. With Your help I desire to make everything I do a carefully chosen practice rather than an unthinking habit.

HOW BIG IS YOUR FAITH?

*"Truly I tell you, if you have faith as small
as a mustard seed, you can say to this mountain,
'Move from here to there,' and it will move.
Nothing will be impossible for you."*

MATTHEW 17:20 NIV

Lord Jesus, I often wonder if I have enough faith—a big enough faith to believe You for the great things You've promised to do for me. So I remain stuck in the same place, afraid that You'll be offended at my small faith. But You tell me that I don't need a lot of faith to do great things for You, or to have You do great things for me. All I need to do is move out in the faith I have and ask. Remind me daily that the issue isn't the size of my faith but the greatness of my God.

Day 106

★ FORGIVING OTHERS ★

*For thou, Lord, art good, and ready
to forgive; and plenteous in mercy
unto all them that call upon thee.*

PSALM 86:5 KJV

Lord, it is easy to justify my own mistakes. Yet, I find it difficult to cut any slack for others. When I am late to a meeting, I think it is for a good reason. When others are late, I think it is because of their incompetence or lack of commitment to their responsibilities.

Lord, that is the way my thinking often goes, and I know it is not right. Help me to stop accusing others while excusing my own shortcomings. With Your help, I will show others the same tolerance You have shown me. By forgiving others, I accept Your free grace.

GODLY LOVE

*Love is patient, love is kind. It does not envy,
it does not boast, it is not proud. It does not
dishonor others, it is not self-seeking, it is not
easily angered, it keeps no record of wrongs. Love
does not delight in evil but rejoices with the truth.*

1 Corinthians 13:4–6 niv

God of love, You have called me to love others as
You have loved me. I confess that I need Your help
to love like that. I need to be more patient and kind,
and I need to be more humble. I sometimes become
angry at others when they don't treat me the way I
think I deserve, and I hang on to that anger. Help me
in these areas, Lord. Please start by making me less
self-centered and more others-centered. Help me to
love as You love.

IMPATIENCE

*But we glory in tribulations also: knowing
that tribulation worketh patience.*
ROMANS 5:3 KJV

Dear Father, impatience is one of my faults. I am intolerant of delays at work, irritated when family members do not share my urgency, and restless in the face of inaction. Sometimes I impatiently decide You are not going to solve a problem, and I act outside Your will. I make ill-considered decisions and take reckless actions that endanger me physically and spiritually. Father, I trust in You. I pray that Your inner peace will sustain me. My goal is neither the impatience of rash actions nor the inaction of passive resignation, but the endurance of a mature Christian who awaits Your will.

THE PRIVILEGE OF PRAYER

"As for me, far be it from me that I should sin against the LORD in ceasing to pray for you; but I will teach you the good and the right way."

1 SAMUEL 12:23 NKJV

Faithful God, thank You for the gift of prayer. Prayer is a wonderful privilege for the man who loves You, but it's also my responsibility. You have called me to pray for everything that concerns me and everything that concerns You. You want me to pray for myself and my family, for my Christian brothers and sisters, for those who need Jesus, for my nation and its leaders, and anything else You lay on my heart. When I pray, You are moved to change situations and change hearts. Never allow me to neglect daily talks with You—or my listening to hear what You have to say in return.

JUST BEING THERE

*As iron sharpens iron, so a man sharpens
the countenance of his friend.*
PROVERBS 27:17 NKJV

Father in heaven, thank You for the Christian brothers
You've placed in my life. These men mean the world to
me, as they provide me with friendship and fellowship
in You. I know You want me to remain "sharp," and I've
seen how You accomplish that by using my friends to
challenge, confront, and encourage me in my walk of
faith. Remind me to tell them how much I appreciate
the part they play in my walk of faith, and help us
to submit to one another in a mutual relationship of
encouragement and accountability. Make me the kind
of friend who helps keep my brothers sharp in their
walk of faith too.

RESPONDING TO POWER

*But when Daniel learned that the law had been
signed, he went home and knelt down as usual in
his upstairs room, with its windows open toward
Jerusalem. He prayed three times a day, just as he
had always done, giving thanks to his God.*

DANIEL 6:10 NLT

Lord, sometimes I feel shocked at the lack of concern
for You and Your standards in my culture. I am grieved
when I see how people conduct themselves today. I
see many things that bring me to a point of anger or
fear. Please remind me not to dwell on my negative
emotions, but to pray to You about those things that
most concern me. Help me to pray for my culture, for
my political leaders, and for those I know who desperately need Your touch.

KEEPING YOUR WORD

*Above all, my brothers and sisters, do not swear—
not by heaven or by earth or by anything else.
All you need to say is a simple "Yes" or "No."
Otherwise you will be condemned.*

JAMES 5:12 NIV

God of truth, this world puts a lot of value on contracts and oaths. Many men seem to believe that their word means nothing unless it is prefaced with "I swear" or "I promise." Father, I know that's not how it should be with me. I want to be a man people can trust. I want to be a man of my word, a man who always does what he says he will do, a man who tells the whole truth, a man who sees his "Yes" and "No" as completely binding. Make me that kind of man.

TEMPTED TO COMPROMISE

*"If we are thrown into the blazing furnace,
the God we serve is able to deliver us from it. . . .
But even if he does not, we want you to know,
Your Majesty, that we will not serve your gods or
worship the image of gold you have set up."*
DANIEL 3:17–18 NIV

Righteous Father, thank You for this example of men refusing to compromise on what they knew was right. I need their encouragement, because I live in a world that continually pressures me to do things that I know aren't right. When I am faced with a choice between honoring You or compromising my faith, give me the courage to stand for You. Lord, I will serve and obey You and You alone, even when it means encountering all sorts of difficulties.

LAUGHTER

A merry heart doeth good like a medicine:
but a broken spirit drieth the bones.
PROVERBS 17:22 KJV

★   ★   ★

Heavenly Father, I know that You want me to be joyful.
A glad heart cannot help but reveal itself with a ready
smile. How can I feel joy without smiling, and how can
I smile without breaking out in laughter? Although
there are times to be somber, I realize that reacting to
every event with the utmost seriousness can produce
a joyless life. May I never present myself with exagger-
ated dignity. Father, as a joy-filled person, may I offer an
easy smile and an honest laugh that encourage people
to spend time in my presence. I pray I will always have
a joyful outlook that lightens my life and the lives of
those around me.

THE TWO GREATEST COMMANDMENTS

He answered, "'Love the Lord your God with all
your heart and with all your soul and with all
your strength and with all your mind'; and,
'Love your neighbor as yourself.'"
LUKE 10:27 NIV

Lord Jesus, You came to earth to bring a message of love. You demonstrated Your love for God and for people through Your words, Your actions, and even Your prayers. Your Word tells me that my love—love for You and for other people—isn't just to be emotional and verbal, but from the heart and accompanied by actions. Lord, I want to love God and other people the way You loved them. I want to live my life in a way that shows the true value of the two greatest commandments. May I reflect my love for You in everything I do, say, and pray.

STRENGTH AND COURAGE FROM ABOVE

*"Be strong and courageous. Do not
be afraid or terrified because of them,
for the LORD your God goes with you;
he will never leave you nor forsake you."*

DEUTERONOMY 31:6 NIV

★　★　★

Lord, sometimes I feel weak and afraid. Sometimes I'm overwhelmed, and I wonder how I'll ever truly enjoy the abundant life You've promised me. Life is often difficult, and it seems like the problems it throws my way are much too big for me. But I take courage in knowing that You are the all-powerful God who promises never to leave me to fight alone. While I'm limited in what I can do, nothing is too hard for You. I need the peace and the empowerment You've promised those who love and follow You.

SYNERGY

Be of the same mind one toward another.
Mind not high things, but condescend to men
of low estate. Be not wise in your own conceits.
ROMANS 12:16 KJV

★ ★ ★

Lord, wonderful moments occur when I work so well with another person that we seem to act as one individual. Our ideas function perfectly together, and our progress toward our goal goes more quickly than our individual efforts would. We have a shared objective, and we use our different talents to accomplish our unified purpose. Father, please help me recognize that differences between people are not negative but positive. Give me the insight to see how I can harmonize with them to make a pleasing whole. Guide me to be a cooperative individual as I work within Your kingdom.

KNOW YOUR ENEMY

Be alert and of sober mind. Your enemy the devil prowls around like a roaring lion looking for someone to devour. Resist him, standing firm in the faith, because you know that the family of believers throughout the world is undergoing the same kind of sufferings.

1 PETER 5:8–9 NIV

★　★　★

Father in heaven, thank You for giving me a heads-up about the enemy of my soul, the devil. He loves to use lies and temptations to distract and derail me in my walk with You. He knows that I am Yours forever, so now he works overtime to keep me from the work You've given me to do. Lord, give me the insight and wisdom to know when the devil is lying in wait for me, so I may avoid him and remain on-track for You.

⎯⎯ A LIVING SACRIFICE ⎯⎯

And so, dear brothers and sisters, I plead with you to give your bodies to God because of all he has done for you. Let them be a living and holy sacrifice—the kind he will find acceptable. This is truly the way to worship him.

ROMANS 12:1 NLT

Father in heaven, I confess that the idea of presenting everything—including my very physical body—to You can be frightening. I have to admit that I've often given You less of myself than You deserve. I guess my fears come from the unknown. What do You want to do with me? Where will You send me? What will You ask me to give up for Your kingdom? Ease my apprehensions and help me to focus on the fact that You love me and want to bless me when I give my everything for Your use.

Day 120

★ LIVING WORDS ★

*And thou shalt teach them diligently unto thy
children, and shalt talk of them when thou sittest
in thine house, and when thou walkest by the way,
and when thou liest down, and when thou risest up.*

DEUTERONOMY 6:7 KJV

Father, I know that You call upon me to teach my children Your Law. It is easy for me to tell my children what
to do if I think I do not have to do it myself. Father, help
me be like Jesus, who illustrated His powerful sermons
with examples of love, compassion, and humility. I want
my children to receive good training by examples of
my actions. May I demonstrate Your love in my daily
routine. Lord, write Your commandments on my life so
they will be a living lesson to my children.

A HEART FOR FORGIVENESS

*"For if you forgive other people when they sin
against you, your heavenly Father will also
forgive you. But if you do not forgive others their
sins, your Father will not forgive your sins."*
MATTHEW 6:14–15 NIV

My gracious heavenly Father, forgiveness is so important to You that You sent Your Son to earth to die so that my sins could be forgiven. Forgiveness is so important to You that You require me to forgive others before You forgive me. I confess that I sometimes have a tough time forgiving others. It's easy for me to hang on to offenses and dwell on them. Forgive me for my unforgiveness, and give me a heart like Yours—a heart that *wants* to forgive others when they do things that hurt or offend me.

THE PERIL OF LOVING MONEY

But those who desire to be rich fall into temptation and a snare, and into many foolish and harmful lusts which drown men in destruction and perdition. For the love of money is a root of all kinds of evil, for which some have strayed from the faith in their greediness, and pierced themselves through with many sorrows.

1 TIMOTHY 6:9–10 NKJV

Father in heaven, I've seen so many people destroy their lives, and the lives of others, by their love of money. Lord, You never condemned money itself as evil, and You actually encourage men to work hard to earn a living. But too many of us make money an object of love rather than a tool to care for our families and fund Your work. Empower me to work hard to earn, but keep my heart from the love of money.

ASKING FOR A MIRACLE

Jesus said to him, "If you can believe, all things are possible to him who believes." Immediately the father of the child cried out and said with tears, "Lord, I believe; help my unbelief!"

MARK 9:23–24 NKJV

Lord Jesus, I've read the Bible stories of You performing amazing miracles during Your earthly ministry, and I've heard many modern-day stories of incidents that can only be explained as being Your work. I don't doubt for a minute that You have the power to perform miracles on behalf of people who cry out to You. Where I often struggle, though, is believing that You will perform a miracle for *me*. Thank You for loving me and making me one of Your own. I love You and believe You, Jesus, but help my unbelief. I need a miracle today.

LOVING THE UNLOVABLE

*If your enemy is hungry, give him food to eat;
if he is thirsty, give him water to drink. In doing
this, you will heap burning coals on his head,
and the LORD will reward you.*

PROVERBS 25:21–22 NIV

Lord Jesus, You once asked Your followers, "If you love those who love you, what reward will you get?" The answer must have been "none"—because You wanted the disciples to understand that, as Your followers, they should do good for those who didn't love them in return. I confess that something inside me recoils at the thought of doing good for someone who won't appreciate it—someone who doesn't care about me. Lord, remind me every day that You call me to love everyone equally—even those who dislike or mistreat me.

THE RIGHT KIND OF BOASTING

*"Let not the wise boast of their wisdom or
the strong boast of their strength or the rich
boast of their riches, but let the one who boasts
boast about this: that they have the understanding
to know me, that I am the LORD, who exercises
kindness, justice and righteousness on earth,
for in these I delight," declares the LORD.*

JEREMIAH 9:23–24 NIV

Lord, remind me daily that I have nothing in and of
myself to boast about. I know that even my understanding and knowledge of You come not from my own heart
or mind but because I have Your Holy Spirit in me.
When I boast, let me boast of You, never of myself. Let
me boast of Your kindness and righteousness, which
are the very reason You saved me in the first place.

GROWING IN FORGIVENESS

For thus saith the LORD of hosts; After the glory hath he sent me unto the nations which spoiled you: for he that toucheth you toucheth the apple of his eye.

ZECHARIAH 2:8 KJV

Heavenly Father, I am struck by references in the Old Testament that describe Your people as the apple of Your eye. I realize that I am very precious in Your sight. If I am the apple of Your eye, then I must replicate Your characteristics to be a true offspring of Yours, just as apples reproduce seeds like those from which they originated. Lord, since I am Your offspring, I need to compare my righteousness to You and not to others. Help me to grow in Your likeness by freely forgiving the offenses of others.

AN ETERNAL HOME

"My Father's house has many rooms; if that were not so, would I have told you that I am going there to prepare a place for you? And if I go and prepare a place for you, I will come back and take you to be with me that you also may be where I am."

JOHN 14:2–3 NIV

★ ★ ★

Lord Jesus, as You hung dying on a cross of wood, You took the time to offer an amazing promise to a penitent criminal: "Today, you will be with me in paradise." When I consider the fact that those words came from the Creator of the universe, my mind spins. What will my eternal home look like? Thank You for preparing a place especially for me, a place that will be an eternal paradise.

HEAVENLY TREASURES

"Do not lay up for yourselves treasures on earth, where moth and rust destroy and where thieves break in and steal; but lay up for yourselves treasures in heaven, where neither moth nor rust destroys and where thieves do not break in and steal. For where your treasure is, there your heart will be also."

MATTHEW 6:19–21 NKJV

Loving Savior, most men I know measure success in terms of what they can accumulate for themselves—the big bank account, the spacious home, the nice cars. But You have told me that those things will mean nothing when I enter into eternity. What will count then is how I've served You here on this earth. I know I need to work and earn a living in this life. But remind me daily to focus on storing up treasure—incorruptible, eternal treasure—with You in heaven.

GET OVER IT

And when ye stand praying, forgive, if ye have ought against any: that your Father also which is in heaven may forgive you your trespasses.

MARK 11:25 KJV

Sometimes, Lord, my mind wanders back to earlier in my life. For some reason, injustices come to mind more readily than pleasant experiences. Anger surfaces when I dwell on the unfair treatment I experienced. I had many privileged opportunities and blessings, but I remember the negative events with far more emotion than the positive occasions.

Forgiving Lord, help me press on with my life. Reviewing reruns of my past serves no purpose. I will not use past events as an excuse for my current shortcomings. With Your help, I will release the resentments I am carrying and accept responsibility for my own actions.

GOOD FOR THE SOUL

*How can I know all the sins lurking in
my heart? Cleanse me from these hidden
faults. Keep your servant from deliberate
sins! Don't let them control me. Then I will
be free of guilt and innocent of great sin.*

PSALM 19:12–13 NLT

Father in heaven, sometimes I make confessing my
sins to You more complicated than it needs to be. I
know that You take great pleasure in forgiving me and
cleansing me when I come to You in confession. I also
know that You give me the power to overcome sin so
that it doesn't control me or define me. And I know it's
the only way to bring healing to myself and to others.
Lord, I echo David's prayer: show me the things I need
to confess, especially the ones I'm not even conscious
of. I want to start my day on solid ground with You.

A TRUSTWORTHY HEAVENLY FATHER

*See what great love the Father has
lavished on us, that we should be called
children of God! And that is what we are!*

1 JOHN 3:1 NIV

Father God, You have repeatedly identified Yourself in scripture as a loving heavenly Father, one I can fully trust to love me as a valued son. Some men struggle with the idea of the Creator of the world also being a loving Father—maybe because their earthly fathers were not good models of what love should look like. But Your love is far deeper and broader than that of even the best earthly father. You are perfect in every way, including in Your love for Your children. Thank You for being a loving heavenly Father—*my* loving heavenly Father.

GOD'S WONDERFUL CREATION

I will praise thee, O LORD, with my whole heart;
I will shew forth all thy marvellous works.
I will be glad and rejoice in thee: I will sing
praise to thy name, O thou most High.

PSALM 9:1–2 KJV

Dear Lord, during the early morning of a day I spent in the desert, insects crawled into the blossoms of a hedgehog cactus. At midday, a red-tailed hawk rested on a tall saguaro and watched for an incautious lizard to dart from its shade beneath a rock. Late in the evening I observed a hungry coyote eating fruit that had dropped to the ground from a date palm.

Father God, I watched in fascination as life managed to survive and even thrive despite the harsh environment. I rejoiced in the wonder that I saw in Your created earth. May I too survive and thrive in Your love.

GOD IS THE ONLY PROVIDER

*"When you enter the land I am going to give you
and you reap its harvest, bring to the priest a sheaf
of the first grain you harvest. . . . You must not eat
any bread, or roasted or new grain, until the very
day you bring this offering to your God."*

LEVITICUS 23:9, 14 NIV

Father in heaven, I know that You've given me everything I have. You've enabled me to earn what I need
to take care of myself and my family. But sometimes I
forget that You are my Source for everything. I'm often
slow to remember You and to thank You when things
are going well. Forgive me for losing sight of these
truths, for losing sight of You. Remind me regularly
that any success I enjoy is Your doing and a result of
Your generosity toward me. Lord, let me never seek or
accept the credit for what You alone have provided.

A SOBER REMINDER

Don't be so naive and self-confident. You're not exempt. You could fall flat on your face as easily as anyone else. Forget about self-confidence; it's useless. Cultivate God-confidence.

1 CORINTHIANS 10:12 MSG

Lord, Your Word warns me against trusting in myself and my own abilities. I know that if I fall into that trip, I am all the more vulnerable to sin. May never become self-confident or pat myself on the back when I feel like I'm doing well. Instead, help me to cultivate confidence in You and in Your ability to keep me from falling. Help me to live a life of obedience and joy in You. Empower me to walk in Your Spirit when times get tough so that my trust in You increases. Help me to see with spiritual eyes so I can always stay the course.

STANDING STRONG

When Saul realized that the LORD was with David and that his daughter Michal loved David, Saul became still more afraid of him, and he remained his enemy the rest of his days.

1 SAMUEL 18:28–29 NIV

Lord, sometimes life is unnerving. I often face situations at work and in other areas of my life when others don't have my best interests in mind. Sometimes people try to make my life difficult just because I follow You. I'm sometimes tempted to lay low and stay quiet about what I believe, but I know that wouldn't honor You— and it would keep me from reaching others with Your wonderful plan for salvation. Grant me the courage and strength to represent You well, even when people around me don't honor Your or want to hear about You.

PRAY FOR OTHERS
WHO SERVE GOD

Paul and Barnabas appointed elders for them in each church and, with prayer and fasting, committed them to the Lord, in whom they had put their trust.

ACTS 14:23 NIV

Father in heaven, thank You for using Your written word to provide me with great examples of what it looks like to follow You and honor You. Paul and Barnabas, two great men of God, served You and helped others honor You by praying for those You put in positions of leadership. I don't always remember to pray for my pastor or for other leaders in my local church, but I know You want me to do just that—and regularly. Lord, I aspire to be a servant-leader within my family, friends, and local church. More than ever, I trust in You! May I never forget to pray for those You've placed in positions of leadership.

★ BOLD ENOUGH TO ASK ★

*Two blind men were sitting by the roadside,
and when they heard that Jesus was going by,
they shouted, "Lord, Son of David, have mercy on us!"*
MATTHEW 20:30 NIV

Father God, when my life is going well and problems are few, it's easy for me to start thinking that I don't need You as much as I do when I'm struggling. I start thinking that I'm meeting my own needs, so I can just put You in the background until get tough. I know that's not Your plan for me. You want me to walk closely with You—during the good times and during the tough times alike. You want me to see life from Your perspective. May I never forget to call out to You when I feel like I need help. . .or when I am feeling comfortable. May I never forget that You help those who ask for help. May I always be bold enough to ask You for what I need—and what I know You want to give me.

WHEN EXHAUSTION BECOMES FAITH

Hear my cry, O God; attend to my prayer. From the end of the earth I will cry to You, when my heart is overwhelmed; lead me to the rock that is higher than I. For You have been a shelter for me, a strong tower from the enemy. I will abide in Your tabernacle forever; I will trust in the shelter of Your wings.

PSALM 61:1–4 NKJV

★ ★ ★

O God, thank You for giving me examples in Your Word of people who felt some of the same things I sometimes do now. When people You loved expressed their fears, complaints, and disappointments, You listened to them and eased their hearts—even when You didn't change their circumstances. Thank You that I can come into Your presence when life becomes overwhelming, when my heart is near breaking. Father, I cry out to You! Keep me close, and lift me up! You are my refuge! Thank You for being my strong tower and my source of peace!

LIVING WITHIN BORDERS

The LORD said to Moses, "Come up to me on the mountain and stay here, and I will give you the tablets of stone with the law and commandments I have written for their instruction."
EXODUS 24:12 NIV

★ ★ ★

Lord God, like many men, I don't like it when I feel like someone has limited my freedoms. I want to do what I want to do, when I want to do it. But You, Lord, are infinitely wise, and You have put limitations on the things I can do—limitations that are for my own good and for Your glory. You have given me Your commands as borders that keep me close to Your best, and if I go beyond those borders, I'll hurt others, hurt myself, and dishonor You. Lord, help me remember that Your commands are for my protection and not because You want to keep me from things I want. Help me trust that Your best plan requires that I respect boundaries.

THE PROMISE OF
THE HOLY SPIRIT

*"If you love me, obey my commandments. And I
will ask the Father, and he will give you another
Advocate, who will never leave you."*

JOHN 14:15–16 NLT

Lord Jesus, You've promised everyone who loves and
follows You the gift of Your Holy Spirit. You taught
that the Holy Spirit will remain in me and that He will
guide me into truth and empower me to be the man
You've created me to be. But I confess that there are
times in my life when I don't feel His guidance or empowerment. Help me to always remember that living
in Your power starts with simple faith in the promises
You've made to me and all my brothers and sisters in
the faith. I can't earn the gift of the Holy Spirit any
more than I can earn my salvation. It's a gift, a gift You
have graciously extended to Your followers. Those who
seek, will find. Make me a faithful seeker!

NOT ALWAYS REWARDED IMMEDIATELY

"I am blameless before God; I have kept myself from sin. The LORD rewarded me for doing right. He has seen my innocence."

2 SAMUEL 22:24–25 NLT

Father in heaven, my fallen human side is prone to wandering into places You don't want me to be and doing things You don't want me to do. But I know You love me enough to help me to keep from sinning against You. I know that You bless me when I do the things You want me to do, and avoid doing the things You've told me not to do. Lord, help me to live a life that pleases You in every way. I ask You to help me to remain committed to glorifying You and following You closely no matter what. I know that my obedience and faithfulness today will one day return to me as a blessing.

═══ LIVE IN PEACE ═══

Finally, brethren, farewell. Become complete. Be of good comfort, be of one mind, live in peace; and the God of love and peace will be with you.
2 CORINTHIANS 13:11 NKJV

★ ★ ★

Father, I know You want me to be at peace with my brothers and sisters in the faith. Sometimes, though, I feel the need to voice my disagreements over smaller matters of theology—things that just aren't worth arguing over. Lord, I know there will be times when I need to speak up when I see or hear serious error. Give me the wisdom to know when I should take a stand, and when I should just agree with someone to disagree . . .while keeping the peace You've called us to live in. Remind me of this important command the next time I butt heads with a fellow believer over an issue that really is of no consequence in Your eternal kingdom.

WHO HAS GOD
ENTRUSTED TO YOU?

*It was soon evident that God had entrusted me
with the same message to the non-Jews as
Peter had been preaching to the Jews.*

GALATIANS 2:7 MSG

Lord Jesus, when You saved me, You gave me the
privilege of representing You in front of people You've
placed in my life. My Savior, I want to be open to
reaching anyone at any time, including people who
don't look like me, talk like me, or even think like me.
You've placed within me a burden for people who
need You. Show me who You want me to reach and
how I can best reach them. Of course, I want to be
available to all, but I know that You often equip men
who know You to reach a specific people group. Here
I am, Lord! Use me!

═ DON'T WASTE AN OPPORTUNITY ═

*"The master was full of praise. 'Well done,
my good and faithful servant. You have been
faithful in handling this small amount, so now
I will give you many more responsibilities.'"*

MATTHEW 25:21 NLT

★ ★ ★

Lord, You've given me so much, starting with something I could never have earned on my own: my eternal salvation. But You've also given me the responsibility of giving of myself to others. I want to give. I want to glorify You by using the amazing gifts with which You've entrusted me. I don't want to hoard what You've given me, and I don't want to just sit on my laurels, enjoying Your generosity. You have invested so much in me, and I know You want to see if You can trust me with what You've done for me and given me. Help me to start where I am today, giving to those who are in need. Help me not to hide my gifts and waste the opportunities You give me.

CLOUD AND FIRE TRAINING

*The cloud of the L*ORD *was over the tabernacle by day, and fire was in the cloud by night, in the sight of all the Israelites during all their travels.*
EXODUS 40:38 NIV

Lord God, there was a time in my life when I didn't know You or follow You in any way. Even after You brought me into Your eternal kingdom, there have been times when I didn't follow You as closely as I knew I should. Lord, I blew it, and I disobeyed You and went my own way for a time. Lord, I ask You to forgive me and I ask You to do whatever it takes to keep me on the path You have for me. Father, I'm in the middle of my journey with You, and I know You are still leading me. Each new day brings an opportunity to follow You toward the destination You have for me. Thanks for encouraging me to return from my disobedience. Thanks for considering my life worth the effort. May each decision I make help me follow Your plan.

OVERCOMING "SELF"

*Not that we are sufficient of ourselves to
think of anything as being from ourselves,
but our sufficiency is from God.*
2 CORINTHIANS 3:5 NKJV

Father in heaven, I live in a world where self-sufficiency is seen as a great virtue. It seems that most men take great pride in being able to do for themselves. But the problem with self-sufficiency is *self*. You have taught me that I shouldn't feel sufficient in myself, but in You above all. Lord, I confess that I focus on *self* too much of the time. But when I do that, I find myself burning out and crashing. Lord, I need You. I thank You that You've made me so dependent on You. Help me never to forget that You alone are sufficient for me.

DISCIPLINE FROM A LOVING FATHER

*"As many as I love, I rebuke and chasten.
Therefore be zealous and repent."*
REVELATION 3:19 NKJV

Loving heavenly Father, many things go into being a good father, and one of them is discipline. Your written Word tells me that a father who doesn't correct his children doesn't actually love them as he should. You, Lord, are more than a good Father; You're a *perfect* Father. You're perfect in Your holiness and perfect in Your love, and that's why You discipline every man You call Your son. It can be unpleasant and difficult when Your hand of discipline is upon me, but I can be grateful for those times, for it reminds me to trust in You and in Your intense love for me. I may not enjoy those times when You send discipline my way, but I thank You for them because they're yet another demonstration of Your love for me.

FORGIVE ME, FATHER

Restore to me the joy of your salvation, and make me willing to obey you. Then I will teach your ways to rebels, and they will return to you.

PSALM 51:12–13 NLT

Father God, I don't like feeling distant from You because I've gone off track in some area of my life. I don't like the feeling of losing the joy I'm supposed to experience from belonging to You. I hate feeling disconnected from You because of my own sin and bad choices. I know that You want me to be close to You, but I also know that sin drives a wedge between me and You. Unconfessed sin pushes me further away from You, so help me to quickly recognize when I've blown it. . .and then to come to You seeking restoration. And when that happens, help me to tell others about the joy of Your forgiveness and my fellowship with You.

A BIBLICAL ANATOMY LESSON

*Just as a body, though one, has many
parts, but all its many parts form
one body, so it is with Christ.*
1 CORINTHIANS 12:12 NIV

Father in heaven, I acknowledge that I am a part of
Your greater plan for this world and for Your eternal
kingdom. I thank You that You've made me a part of
the body of Christ and a part of my local congregation.
You never intended for me to attend church services
every week just to warm a pew. On the contrary, You've
given me special gifts and abilities so that I can serve
this wonderful organism called the Body of Christ.
Father God, I want to be a servant to my brothers and
sisters in You. Show me daily how I can use the gifts
You've given me to do just that.

TRUST, NOT CERTAINTY

*In peace I will lie down and sleep,
for you alone, O LORD, will keep me safe.*
PSALM 4:8 NLT

Gracious heavenly Father, You've more than proven Yourself worthy of my trust—both in the examples I see in Your Word and in the things You've done for me as I walk closely with You. I love the peace You give me when I simply rest in You. I love being able to live peacefully and sleep soundly, knowing that You've got everything in control and want to keep me safe. Lord, help me to always trust You instead of my own ability to provide. Thank You that I can call on You for help and vindication because I belong to You. God, I am set apart for Your purposes, and I can ace any challenge, even my prideful tendencies, knowing that You are with me.

CLEANSING THE CONSCIENCE

*Cling to your faith in Christ, and keep
your conscience clear. For some people
have deliberately violated their consciences;
as a result, their faith has been shipwrecked.*

1 TIMOTHY 1:19 NLT

Loving God, I thank You that You've given me a conscience so I can know the things You say are right as well as the things You say are wrong. Lord, when I stray from what You want for me, something inside me tells me that I'm off track. Your Spirit speaks within me, telling me that I need to repent of my sin so I can be right with You. Father, You long to forgive me and set me free. When I confess my sin, You restore me and give me the ability to live an overcoming, victorious life by Your Spirit. Lord, I confess my sins to You, and I forsake them. Help me to accept Your forgiveness and make things right with others, if possible. Help me to live with a clear conscience.

LIGHTING THE DARK

*The night is far spent, the day is at hand:
let us therefore cast off the works of darkness,
and let us put on the armour of light.*
ROMANS 13:12 KJV

Heavenly Father, this valley that I walk in has two different aspects depending on the angle of the sun. In the evening, the shadow of a hill casts the valley into deep gloom. But in the early hours of the day, the valley is bright because it faces the morning sun.

Father, what a difference the sun makes in the natural world, and what a difference when I see my life with the light You provide! When I walk through dark passages in my life, I pray that my eyes will be opened to the illumination that You provide. Give me a positive outlook to overcome the dreary times. Keep me in the light of Your blessings.

GIVING WISE COUNSEL

Behold, God exalteth by his power:
who teacheth like him?
JOB 36:22 KJV

Lord, the opportunity to shape other lives is both a blessing and an awesome responsibility. Show me how to admonish, correct, and inspire those who come to me for guidance, whether it be at work, at church, or in the community. Help me build relationships founded on trust.

Lord, no one teaches like You; regardless of the circumstances, I pray I will ground my advice in Your Word. Give me the dedication and calm self-assurance to help the people I am mentoring realize higher objectives for their lives. I pray that they will have the conviction to remain on course when I am no longer guiding them.

BEYOND SELF

Not that I speak in respect of want:
for I have learned, in whatsoever
state I am, therewith to be content.

PHILIPPIANS 4:11 KJV

Sometimes, Lord, I pray with a selfish agenda. I pray for a new job with better pay. I ask for a new house. I beg for a new truck. When I focus on my wants and not on my needs, I realize my priorities are misplaced. I forget to look upward to seek Your will for my life. All-knowing God, You see the larger picture, and You have the best interest for my future in view. Teach me, Lord, to keep my eyes on You and then to look outward and extend a hand to those who are truly in need.

TRUST IN THE LORD

Trust in the LORD with all thine heart;
and lean not unto thine own understanding.
PROVERBS 3:5 KJV

Father, on the way to work I saw a high-rise office building under construction. At dizzying heights, the workers appeared unconcerned as they walked on narrow ribbons of steel. That is something I could not do. Yet, set the same steel beam a few inches above the ground, and I could walk across it without concern.

Father, when I am apprehensive about tasks that need to be done, remind me that Your protective hand is over me. I pray that I will learn to step out in faith, secure in the knowledge that You are there for me.

SHARPENING THE SAW

I have taught thee in the way of wisdom;
I have led thee in right paths.
PROVERBS 4:11 KJV

Lord, even after I sharpened my chain saw, it still wasn't cutting too well. When the chain came off, I realized the problem—I had put the chain on backwards. Father, in my business life, my personal life, and my spiritual life, I understand the importance of investing in myself. I need to learn new skills, try different approaches, and improve myself physically, mentally, and spiritually. But a sharp saw is not enough. Even after I hone my talents, I must use them properly. May I always use them in a way that reaps the most benefit for Your kingdom.

WHAT UPSETS YOU?

For the flesh lusteth against the Spirit,
and the Spirit against the flesh: and these
are contrary the one to the other: so that
ye cannot do the things that ye would.
GALATIANS 5:17 KJV

Heavenly Counselor, I encounter many problems each day. Sometimes they arise from the simple struggles of daily life, like a car with a dead battery or a home with a faulty hot water tank. Keep me from becoming upset because of inanimate objects. Sometimes I have conflicts with people whose business objectives are different from mine. Help me refuse to act improperly in daily give-and-take with others. I too struggle with my own limitations, like forgetfulness. May I never become frustrated by my lack of proficiency.

Father, one conflict I especially want to avoid is one with the Holy Spirit. May I never work against Your purposes.

CONTENTMENT

Now godliness with contentment is great gain.
For we brought nothing into this world, and it is
certain we can carry nothing out. And having food
and clothing, with these we shall be content.

1 TIMOTHY 6:6–8 NKJV

God of light, I confess that if I'm not careful, I can place too much attention on acquiring earthly wealth and possessions. Your Word never condemns financial or material gain, but it does tell me I should never place my desire for those things over my desire for You. Lord, You want me to live a life of godliness and contentment. You want me to focus on conduct, thoughts, and attitudes that reflect You best. Lord, let me be content with all You've given me. Please help me always to pursue You and the life You want me to live.

TRUST IN HIS DEFENSE

*But let all those that put their trust in
thee rejoice: let them ever shout for joy,
because thou defendest them: let them
also that love thy name be joyful in thee.*

Psalm 5:11 kjv

Thankfully, dear Jesus, I have never been falsely accused of a crime and had to stand trial. Should that unfortunate event occur, I would want a skilled defense attorney to plead my case and believable witnesses to establish my innocence.

Lord, the Bible says that You defend those who believe in You. When Satan brings charges against my life or character, I am encouraged that You are my defense attorney and also my witness. Thank You for accepting my faith and trust as the evidence You need to render the verdict, "Not guilty! Case closed!"

PAGES OF TIME

Let not mercy and truth forsake thee:
bind them about thy neck; write them
upon the table of thine heart.
PROVERBS 3:3 KJV

Lord, with my smartphone, I can specify the subjects that are displayed on my screen. I can choose the news content, weather report, financial statements, sports scores, and entertainment guide. I can personalize it to my taste.

Father, today You have given me a fresh page of my life. I can write upon it words that encourage or words that destroy, acts of kindness or selfish deeds, thoughts that cause my spirit to soar or ideas that bring me low. Let me wisely choose the content of my life to glorify You.

ASKING IN JESUS' NAME

*"I will do whatever you ask in my name, so that
the Father may be glorified in the Son. You may
ask me for anything in my name, and I will do it."*
JOHN 14:13–14 NIV

Lord Jesus, thank You for Your promise to do whatever
I ask in Your name. I confess that if I'm not careful, the
requests I bring can become self-centered. Please keep
me focused on what glorifies my Father in heaven.
Help me to pray for what I know is important to You.
Lord, may I never come to You in prayer with selfish
motives. May I present my requests in Your name for
those things that help me to live the life You call me
to live. . .so that You will be glorified in everything I do.

RESPONSIBILITY

*While we look not at the things which are seen,
but at the things which are not seen: for the
things which are seen are temporal; but the
things which are not seen are eternal.*

2 CORINTHIANS 4:18 KJV

Father, when I was young, some people would excuse their failures or belittle someone else's successes by saying, "In a hundred years no one will remember this." Now that comment allows me to contrast trivial and important matters. Significant comments and actions have a way of reaching beyond the present and affecting eternity. Lord, let me never take lightly my responsibility to dedicate my words and actions to You. Use what I say and do to influence someone to seek eternity with You in heaven. Today I trust that I have done all I could for You.

SETTING A COURSE

What man is he that feareth the LORD?
him shall he teach in the way that he shall choose.
PSALM 25:12 KJV

Lord, I watch the rain and see two raindrops fall only inches apart: one flows to the right, the other flows to the left.

Unlike the raindrops, I have the liberty to choose which direction my life flows. Heavenly Father, keep me from making careless judgments that can develop into frightful consequences. Guide me to choices that lead away from the darkness of sin and into the light of righteousness. Give me Your wisdom as I make choices. I pray that my decisions are based on the values instilled in me by studying Your Word.

★ A DIVINE MASTER ★

*But without faith it is impossible to
please him: for he that cometh to God
must believe that he is, and that he is a
rewarder of them that diligently seek him.*

HEBREWS 11:6 KJV

Lord, there is a bronze statue in Edinburgh, Scotland, that commemorates a Skye terrier named Greyfriars Bobby. After his owner died, this dog followed the funeral procession to the churchyard where they buried his master. The terrier stayed near the grave for the next fourteen years.

Divine Master, when You died, You died because of my sins. I want to dedicate my life to You. I will show my loyalty by being faithful to Your Church and devoted to my family. My eyes will remain fixed on Calvary. Your Cross demonstrates the truth that You will never leave me or forsake me.

DRIVING ON HIGH BEAM

Let your light so shine before men,
that they may see your good works,
and glorify your Father which is in heaven.
MATTHEW 5:16 KJV

Father, when I am driving in the country late at night, I am thankful to have the brilliant high-beam headlights to warn me of deer that might wander onto the road. The focused, concentrated light gives me advance warning of any dangers ahead of me. Dear Jesus, You gave Your disciples the responsibility of living as lights to guide the lost to You. Let Your heavenly beams shine through my life to reveal You as the Savior of the world and to focus praise on the Father. Help me to be diligent in illuminating the narrow road that leads to heaven.

FULLY ARMORED

Put on the whole armour of God, that ye may
be able to stand against the wiles of the devil.
Ephesians 6:11 KJV

Father, when I first gave my life to You, I hungered for Your Word. Every day I read the Bible and studied it carefully. Now my mind strays as I read, and I have to double back and reread passages to comprehend them. I question how much my mind retains and wonder what benefits I am receiving. Yet, each day I eat meals so my body has food to repair tissues and provide energy for physical activities.

In the same way, I understand that reading Your Word provides food for my soul. Lord, I pray that I will always be so hungry for Your Word that I will set aside time for daily Bible reading.

YOUR REAL BATTLE

For our struggle is not against flesh and blood,
but against the rulers, against the authorities,
against the powers of this dark world and against
the spiritual forces of evil in the heavenly realms.

EPHESIANS 6:12 NIV

All-powerful God, it's easy for me to think of people who stand against You and Your standards as my enemies. But You warn me that my true enemies are the devil and his spiritual minions, who will typically attack me where I'm weakest. Lord, I know that You tell me this as a warning so I can stand against the one who wishes me harm. I'm in a battle, Father, against an enemy I can't stand against on my own. But I know You are with me, and You have given me weapons not only to defend myself but to emerge victorious.

SPIRITUAL DEFENSE SYSTEMS

Therefore put on the full armor of God, so that when the day of evil comes, you may be able to stand your ground, and after you have done everything, to stand. Stand firm then, with the belt of truth buckled around your waist, with the breastplate of righteousness in place, and with your feet fitted with the readiness that comes from the gospel of peace.
EPHESIANS 6:13–15 NIV

God of power and might, the Bible tells me that being a Christian on this side of eternity means going to war against spiritual forces. They work around the clock to keep people from knowing You and joining Your eternal kingdom. These same forces try to tempt me and other believers to sin—or at least to live a distracted life. But with the weapons of truth, righteousness, and readiness at my disposal, no spiritual enemy coming against me can succeed.

═══ A WEAPON OF OFFENSE ═══

In addition to all this, take up the shield of faith,
with which you can extinguish all the flaming arrows
of the evil one. Take the helmet of salvation and the
sword of the Spirit, which is the word of God.

Ephesians 6:16–17 niv

Lord Jesus, You've given me an overwhelming arsenal of weapons with which I can do spiritual battle. But one of those weapons is different from the others. The Bible calls itself "the sword of the Spirit," and it's the only one of those weapons that is offensive in nature. Remind me regularly that Your written Word is as powerful today as it was in Your days on earth, when You used it to repel the devil's temptations at the beginning of Your ministry.

Day 170

A PERSONAL PRAYER

*And this is life eternal, that they
might know thee the only true God,
and Jesus Christ, whom thou hast sent.*
JOHN 17:3 KJV

Heavenly Father, in this prayer I want to speak to You about myself. I pray that it is not a selfish prayer, for my ultimate goal is to be right with You. Please make a way for me to avoid sin and help me to accept Your forgiveness when I do sin. I long to be right with You. Direct my steps to always be in the path of righteousness.

Father, help me recognize the work You have given me to do, and assist me as I try to glorify You. Stamp Your name on my heart so that I may live eternally in Your presence.

OPEN-DOOR POLICY

*Thou shalt guide me with thy counsel,
and afterward receive me to glory.*
PSALM 73:24 KJV

★ ★ ★

Lord, I once had a supervisor who had an open-door policy. Whenever I was torn about the best course of action to solve a problem, I would spend a few minutes talking with him. Sometimes he would suggest an option; sometimes he would caution me against an option. I am thankful, Father, that You have an open-door policy. I can talk to You day or night about the things that trouble me. It is a comfort to know that You are there to listen. I know that You will make clear to me the correct decision.

LISTENING

Be still, and know that I am God:
I will be exalted among the heathen,
I will be exalted in the earth.
PSALM 46:10 KJV

★　★　★

Sometimes, Lord, training merely makes me feel bad because after learning what I should do, I realize that I fall far short of perfection. For example, to communicate well, I should listen first. But rather than listening, I am sometimes merely exercising patience while waiting to talk. I should be attentive with my whole mind and body, and I should exchange ideas as well as words. Father, please help me use my best listening skills when I come before You. Give me the patience to wait for Your message. Help me not be so anxious to put what I consider urgent matters before You first. May I tune in to You with my mind and heart.

THE LORD'S ANOINTED

*"No!" David said. "Don't kill him.
For who can remain innocent after
attacking the LORD's anointed one?"*
1 SAMUEL 26:9 NLT

Lord, I confess that I don't always mind my tongue when it comes to leaders, but I haven't considered the fact that they, like Saul—in spite of all their flaws—are Your anointed. Forgive me, Lord. Help me to set a better example to others going forward. Remind me to pray daily for national, state, and local leaders—especially when they are leaders I don't agree with on many issues.

SELF-CONTROL

*For this very reason, make every effort to
add to your faith goodness; and to goodness,
knowledge; and to knowledge, self-control.*

2 PETER 1:5–6 NIV

Father, when I sit down to eat, I find it difficult to have self-restraint. Not only do I have problems controlling my appetite for food, but I also have weaknesses in many other areas of my life. Exercising temperance is a challenge. Yet, I know it is a fruit of the Spirit and that I should manifest it in my life. Lord, I ask You to give me power to govern my thoughts and my actions. I pray for moderation and self-restraint in my personal conduct.

RESCUE ME, LORD

In your distress you called and I rescued
you, I answered you out of a thundercloud;
I tested you at the waters of Meribah.
PSALM 81:7 NIV

Lord, sometimes I can't see any way around my circumstances. Sometimes I don't want to be patient
and persevere. Instead, I just want to gripe. Father,
forgive me for my negative, complaining attitude. Help
me to trust You to meet my needs. I know You to be a
faithful, loving God who is more than willing to send
help when I need it. You know my circumstances. Take
me through them, Lord. Rescue me. . . and then remind
me to glorify You for answering me.

DELIVERANCE FROM CAPTURE

And this I pray. . .that ye may approve things that are excellent; that ye may be sincere and without offence till the day of Christ. Being filled with the fruits of righteousness, which are by Jesus Christ, unto the glory and praise of God.
PHILIPPIANS 1:9–11 KJV

Heavenly Father, spiders spin webs to snare wandering insects. Some of the spider webs are in such obscure locations, I wonder how an insect will ever be trapped. But the spider knows how to capture unsuspecting victims. Father, I know that Satan too catches valuable souls in a web of sin. Often the temptation is placed in an unsuspecting location. Lord, guard my mind, spirit, and body from Satan's lures. Deliver me from the temptations to violate Your laws. Only with Your help can I maintain a holy lifestyle and avoid becoming a victim seized by deception.

FAITH STRETCHING

*When Jesus looked out and saw that a
large crowd had arrived, he said to Philip,
"Where can we buy bread to feed these
people?" He said this to stretch Philip's faith.
He already knew what he was going to do.*

JOHN 6:5–6 MSG

Lord Jesus, I confess that the idea of You testing my
faith makes me a little uncomfortable. But I'm willing
to endure whatever test You send my way, knowing
that You love me and want me to grow in my relationship with You. I don't always see with spiritual eyes.
I allow everyday concerns to keep me from trusting
Your miracle-working power. But Your Word teaches
me that You sometimes allow those You love to face
needs and problems in order to stretch their faith. Do
as You will with me, Lord!

FOOT-WASHING

"You call me 'Teacher' and 'Lord,' and you are right, because that's what I am. And since I, your Lord and Teacher, have washed your feet, you ought to wash each other's feet."

JOHN 13:13–14 NLT

★ ★ ★

Lord Jesus, I confess that I'm a lot like Your disciples. I tend to believe that being a leader or one entrusted with big responsibilities means being more like a boss than a servant. But You want me to lead—at home, at church, at work—by selflessly serving those You've placed in my life. I love You, Lord, and I love the people You've put in my world. Help me to have a heart that wants to serve them, and show me ways I can serve today and every day.

GLORIFYING GOD'S NAME

Help us, O God of our salvation, for the glory
of Your name; and deliver us, and provide
atonement for our sins, for Your name's sake!
PSALM 79:9 NKJV

Lord, I confess to being quick to ask for deliverance and slow to being willing to endure affliction, even when it is a result of my own sin. When I'm in a bad place—spiritually, relationally, or physically—help me to examine myself to see if there's something You want to correct. Help me to glorify Your name, regardless of whether or not You choose to deliver me from my afflictions.

SOFTENING THE HARD HEART

*Sow for yourselves righteousness; reap in mercy;
break up your fallow ground, for it is time to seek the
LORD, till He comes and rains righteousness on you.*

HOSEA 10:12 NKJV

Thank You, Lord, for the message of Hosea 10:12. It
looks like advice for a farmer, but it makes the point
that I should take time to earnestly seek You and ask
if I've neglected You in any way. Lord, I need to grow
in my faith, and the only way for that to happen is
for You to soften my heart. Then, as I seek You in prayer
and Bible reading, I can receive what You have for
me. Thank You for hearing me when I ask You to show
me those areas of my life in which I've neglected You.

═══ SUFFERING FOR JESUS ═══

*For you have been given not only the
privilege of trusting in Christ but also
the privilege of suffering for him.*
PHILIPPIANS 1:29 NLT

Lord, I don't like the idea of suffering for anything
or anybody, including You. But my love for You and
for others makes me willing to do just that when it is
required. I know it's not likely that I'll experience the
kind of trials the first-century Christians suffered. All
the same, when I am called to suffer through twenty-
first century trials and tests because of my faith, help
me to see it as a blessed privilege. Help me to continue trusting in You so I can get through my difficulties in a way that glorifies You and helps others to see
Jesus in me.

NEW LIFE

*A good man leaveth an inheritance
to his children's children.*
PROVERBS 13:22 KJV

★ ★ ★

Father, as I hold my newborn son and watch him sleep in peace, I cannot help but wonder what the future holds. A lot is expected of me—and of him. He will carry my name and represent me by extending my hopes beyond what I have accomplished.

Dear Lord, I pray I will give him the freedom to find his own way but also ground him in the essentials of Your Word. I pray that he will inherit from me a name that he will be pleased to wear. But more than anything, I pray that I will see his name written beside mine in the Book of Life.

SUPPLICATION

Be careful for nothing; but in every thing by
prayer and supplication with thanksgiving let
your requests be made known unto God.

PHILIPPIANS 4:6 KJV

Father, I am aware of many people who are suffering and who are in difficult situations. I pray that they and their families will be able to work out the difficulty. Help me to find a way to ease their burden.

I pray also for those people who live lives of quiet desperation—those who never reveal their distress but suffer in silent hopelessness. I pray that I will be sensitive to these individuals, recognize their concerns, and take action to relieve them of the suffering they are trying to bear by themselves.

ROOTED IN THE GOOD SOIL

My son, keep thy father's commandment,
and forsake not the law of thy mother.
PROVERBS 6:20 KJV

Heavenly Father, I hope that my son will develop worthy characteristics as he grows and matures. I pray that he will become a person devoted to honest effort. May he expend his efforts on problems worthy of attack. Should he fail, may it be because he aimed too high rather than accepted defeat too readily. Lord, I cannot ask my son to meet these goals unless I first develop them in myself. My advice will only take root if I plant it in the soil of my own good example. Teach me to choose the honorable path when I am confronted with truth and lies, courage and flight, humility and conceit.

═══ OUR SOURCE OF WISDOM ═══

If any of you lacks wisdom, you should ask God, who gives generously to all without finding fault, and it will be given to you. But when you ask, you must believe and not doubt, because the one who doubts is like a wave of the sea, blown and tossed by the wind.

JAMES 1:5–6 NIV

Lord, I believe it when You say You will generously give me wisdom when I ask for it. I face many life situations that require me to act wisely. Please give me the wisdom to act and speak in ways that glorify You and benefit those You've placed in my life. Today, I choose to trust You to keep Your promise—the promise to give me wisdom when I ask for it. I will leave the "how" up to You.

WEARING A MASK

For the word of God is quick, and powerful, and sharper than any twoedged sword . . .and is a discerner of the thoughts and intents of the heart.

HEBREWS 4:12 KJV

Father, as a child I enjoyed putting on a disguise and pretending to be one of my heroes. Playacting did not end with childhood. As an adult, I modify my behavior to match the situation. My choice of language, how I conduct myself, and the clothes I wear conform to what I imagine will help me fit in with my peers. Stress develops when the image I try to project differs from my true self.

Father, I am always visible to You. May I develop the humility to put off the disguise and work instead toward being the person You want me to be.

VIEW FROM A HEIGHT

For the eyes of the Lord are over the righteous,
and his ears are open unto their prayers.

1 PETER 3:12 KJV

Dear Lord, viewing the world from a thousand feet above it in a hot air balloon gives me an unusual perspective. I can see a canoe that will hit rapids around the bend in the stream. I see cars coming toward one another along a country lane, but because of a hill, the drivers can't see each other. My eyes are no sharper than theirs, but I can see objects hidden from them because I have a different vantage point.

Father, I know You have a better viewpoint. You can see into my heart and into my future. You can see what is coming and prepare me for it. Please continue to watch over me.

A BOTTOMLESS WELL

Judge not, and ye shall not be judged:
condemn not, and ye shall not be condemned:
forgive, and ye shall be forgiven.

LUKE 6:37 KJV

Faithful Lord, I pray that my life will not grow useless and unfruitful in Your kingdom. Your love and mercy are wells that never run dry. Graceful Lord, guide me to excuse the faults of others and extend forgiveness to them without resentment. Thank You for casting my sins away without keeping a record of my failures.

PROPER NOURISHMENT

*Anyone who lives on milk, being still an infant,
is not acquainted with the teaching about
righteousness. But solid food is for the mature,
who by constant use have trained themselves
to distinguish good from evil.*

HEBREWS 5:13–14 NIV

Heavenly Father, nearly every waking hour I'm bombarded with images, music, television shows, and movies that can stunt my spiritual growth. Not only that, I can turn on my screens any time of the day and find unsound "Christian" teaching—teaching that doesn't align with Your written Word. Lord, You've walked with me since the day You brought me into Your eternal kingdom. I want more than anything to grow in my relationship with You, but I need Your help. Give me the wisdom to know what is good for me and what keeps me from growing in You.

Day 190

BY HIS POWER

*Humble yourselves in the sight
of the Lord, and he shall lift you up.*
JAMES 4:10 KJV

As I walk along an ocean's shoreline and see the numerous grains of sand, they remind me, gracious Lord, of Your infinite nature. As I listen to the endless crash of the surf against the shore, the pounding of the waves declares Your power. You have authority over the wind and waves. The unseen forces You created bring in the tides and stir up the restless sea.

Father, I am humbled in the presence of Your creation. I acknowledge You as master of my life. I submit my will to You and dedicate myself to honoring Your name and glorifying Your greatness.

YOUR PROVIDER

Ask the LORD for rain in the springtime; it is the LORD who sends the thunderstorms. He gives showers of rain to all people, and plants of the field to everyone.
ZECHARIAH 10:1 NIV

God my provider, few things can stress an individual or a family more than money problems. Lord, I've found myself in a financial place where I wondered how I was going to cover the next month's expenses and then feed my family. Your Son, my Savior, taught that You're the Creator who always feeds the birds—and who values me far more than them. You have created me to relate with You as a son relates to his father, and a good father wants to provide for his children. You're aware of my needs, and You want to meet them. When I'm in a place of financial stress, help me to look beyond my circumstances and trust You as my provider.

DRIFTING ALONG

And said unto them, Why sleep ye?
rise and pray, lest ye enter into temptation.
LUKE 22:46 KJV

★ ★ ★

Lord, I always enjoy going on a canoe trip. As I drift along with my face turned toward the sun and my fingers running through the cool water, I sometimes grow sleepy. Then, suddenly, I become fully awake as my canoe is caught in the roar of rapids.

Lord Jesus, sometimes I find myself drifting in my spiritual journey. My interest in relationships with other Christians weakens, and my interest in sharing the Gospel diminishes. I feel a false sense of security, and I stop paddling toward the safer channel. Awake me, Lord Jesus, and keep me from drifting into the dangers of this world.

FREE TO ACT IN LOVE

But you must be careful so that your freedom does not cause others with a weaker conscience to stumble.

1 CORINTHIANS 8:9 NLT

Precious Savior, I thank You for setting me free from the power of sin and death. Thank You that I am free to live without constant worry about what is right and wrong in Your eyes. You let me know when I'm on the right track, and You let me know when I need to make changes. But never let me forget that I must make my life choices with an eye toward loving others—especially my brothers in the faith. I never want to be a stumbling block to those with a more sensitive conscience or who are prone to falling back into old sinful behavior.

YOUR WORDS AND THOUGHTS

*May these words of my mouth and
this meditation of my heart be pleasing in
your sight, LORD, my Rock and my Redeemer.*

PSALM 19:14 NIV

Precious God, I confess that my words and my thoughts aren't always of the kind that please You. Sometimes I think negative thoughts about others, including Your own people, and the negative words soon follow. Other times I speak words of complaint about other people's actions, and those words only reinforce my critical, negative thoughts. Lord, I know that my words and my thoughts are connected with one another, so I ask You to help me as I try to speak in ways that build others up—and think thoughts that focus on You and Your Word. I want to please You in all that I say and think.

FORGIVING AS GOD FORGIVES

Bear with each other and forgive one another
if any of you has a grievance against someone.
Forgive as the Lord forgave you.
COLOSSIANS 3:13–14 NIV

Lord Jesus, as You hung on the cross, bloodied and bruised from the beatings You had taken at the hands of Your executioners, You set an example for me. You showed what You expect from me when You said, "Father, forgive them, for they do not know what they are doing." I have a hard time understanding that level of forgiveness. In fact, I struggle to forgive those who have wronged me in even the smallest ways. But that's exactly what You tell me to do, Lord. You've forgiven me for my sins, and You command me to forgive those who sin against me. Please grant me a forgiving heart, for that is the only way I can obey Your command to forgive.

═ TOWARD ETERNITY'S SUNRISE ═

*Therefore my heart is glad, and my glory
rejoiceth: my flesh also shall rest in hope.*
PSALM 16:9 KJV

Heavenly Father, during my morning drive to work, the
day is brighter and the air is cleaner than it was when
I drove home the night before. Each sunrise brings a
fresh day in my spiritual life too. Thank You, Lord, for
releasing me from my past failings so I can face the
day with a glad heart, secure in the knowledge that
Jesus has given me a new start. As I drive on to my
destination during the morning rush, I also desire to
stay on the spiritual highway that leads to my eventual
destination with You.

GIVING CHEERFULLY

*Each of you should give what you have decided
in your heart to give, not reluctantly or under
compulsion, for God loves a cheerful giver.*
2 CORINTHIANS 9:7 NIV

★ ★ ★

Father in heaven, I confess that when I give to causes
that expand Your kingdom and benefit others, I'm not
always as happy as I should be. Sometimes I'm thinking
I might need those funds to care for my own way of
life. But Lord, You want me to give cheerfully, not with
a worried or grudging heart. When I consider what or
how much to give, remind me that giving toward the
work of Your kingdom isn't just a duty but a privilege.
And help me to remember Your promise to care for
my own needs when I give generously.

Day 198

FOR PUBLIC SCHOOLTEACHERS

*A wise man will hear, and will increase
learning; and a man of understanding
shall attain unto wise counsels.*
PROVERBS 1:5 KJV

Heavenly Shepherd, I pray for the schoolteachers of our community. May our educators have the ability to motivate students to their best achievement. Provide them with the means to instill in students a joy for learning and the capacity for a lifetime of seeking the truth. May the teachers be a role model of excellence and integrity.

Develop in our teachers and students the boldness to express love for You. Revive our educational system so teachers and students can express Christian beliefs. May teachers be able to show the religious context that guided the founding of our great nation.

THE REAL ARTICLE

*But the wisdom that is from above is first
pure, then peaceable, gentle, and easy to
be intreated, full of mercy and good fruits,
without partiality, and without hypocrisy.*

JAMES 3:17 KJV

Father, years ago a coworker sold me a gold ring. After a hot and sweaty day, my skin under the ring had turned green. The ring was not pure gold but had only gold plating over copper.

Lord, I pray that my character is not a veneer on the outside. Instead, may the way that I appear on the outside flow from within. Through deliberate effort, I want to develop the attributes—honesty, honor, hospitality, and humility—from which character springs. Father, ensure that the words I say, the actions I take, and the thoughts of my heart are an indivisible combination that reflects a life dedicated to You.

MATURITY

*He is the one we proclaim, admonishing and
teaching everyone with all wisdom, so that we
may present everyone fully mature in Christ.*
COLOSSIANS 1:28 NIV

★ ★ ★

Father God, when I look back to the time You brought
me to salvation and compare that new believer to who
I am today, I can see that You've caused me to mature
in my faith. If I do the same thing in another five years,
I believe I'll see a much more mature Christian man
than I am now. I know that Your will for me is to become
fully mature in You and to help others who are on their
own road to spiritual maturity. Lord, I know I'll only
reach perfection when I'm with You in heaven—but
until then, strengthen me daily as I continue to mature
into the man of God You created me to be.

★ HANDLING REGRETS ★

"So I will restore to you the years that the swarming locust has eaten, the crawling locust, the consuming locust, and the chewing locust."

JOEL 2:25 NKJV

Forgiving God, there are things in my past I'm not proud of, things that make me wince when I think about them. If I could go back to the time in my life before I knew You and do some things differently, I would. But You, Lord, have promised me that You can and do use everything, even my bad decisions in the past, for my good and Your glory. There's nothing I can do to change the past, but there's plenty You can do to teach me important lessons and give me wisdom to impart to others. Lord, remind me always that You are my Redeemer, including the Redeemer of my past.

VOTING WITH YOUR WALLET

For we are his workmanship, created in Christ Jesus unto good works, which God hath before ordained that we should walk in them.
EPHESIANS 2:10 KJV

★   ★   ★

Lord, thank You for the freedom I have to vote for candidates and issues both on the local and national level. I pray for Your guidance in carrying out this responsibility.

Similarly, Lord, I will express my convictions about spiritual issues by the choices I make. Help me be responsible in the causes that I choose to support. Guide me in the purchases I make, the businesses I patronize, and the entertainment venues I attend. Heavenly Father, let every vote I cast, either at the polls or with my wallet, make this country a more righteous nation.

CHOOSING YOUR THOUGHTS

*Finally, brothers and sisters, whatever is
true, whatever is noble, whatever is right,
whatever is pure, whatever is lovely, whatever
is admirable—if anything is excellent or
praiseworthy—think about such things.*

Philippians 4:8 NIV

Father in heaven, it often feels like my thoughts are
out of control, like I am powerless against my worries,
my lusts, and my pride. But You call me to think about
much better things. I'm grateful that You don't call me
to do anything that You don't empower me to do. You've
given me Your written Word to shape my thoughts
and Your Holy Spirit to control them. Thank You for
giving me better things to consider when my mind
goes places that don't help me or glorify You. Thank
You for giving me the ability to focus on higher things.

TAKE WATER AND DRINK IT

But whosoever drinketh of the water that I shall give him shall never thirst; but the water that I shall give him shall be in him a well of water springing up into everlasting life.

JOHN 4:14 KJV

★ ★ ★

Lord, You have designed the human body in such a way that it must have water to survive. We can go without food for several days at a time, but going without water for that long can have disastrous consequences for our bodies. You used that need for water to teach us something about how much we need You too.

I am blessed to have so many ways to learn about Your will. Yet, unless I make the effort to drink in Your Word, I am lost. The Bible says You, Lord Jesus, are the source of water that quenches spiritual thirst. Thank You for granting to me the water that brings life everlasting.

A "NEW" COMMAND

*"A new command I give you: Love one another.
As I have loved you, so you must love one another.
By this everyone will know that you are my
disciples, if you love one another."*

JOHN 13:34–35 NIV

Lord Jesus, during Your earthly ministry, You provided Your followers glimpses of the loving nature of Your heavenly Father—and You taught them the vital importance of loving one another. When You say that Your followers must love one another "as I have loved You," it shows me that You want me to love my spiritual brothers and sisters sacrificially, selflessly, and compassionately. Lord, You never intended Your followers to live self-focused lives, but that is just what I often do. Forgive me, and show me each day how I can love others the way You love me.

TEACHING ABOUT JESUS

These are the things that ye shall do; Speak ye every man the truth to his neighbour; execute the judgment of truth and peace in your gates.
ZECHARIAH 8:16 KJV

Lord Jesus, I occasionally take on the role of teacher, although I often feel inadequate for the task. My goal is to be a mentor, guide, and advisor. May I grow in knowledge, wisdom, character, and confidence so I can help those I teach to choose the proper path.

Heavenly Teacher, provide me with the ability to instill in my students a love for learning more about You, reading the Bible, talking to You in prayer, and living a life in keeping with Your Word. May I have an influence that will last a lifetime.

SEASONING SALT

*Walk in wisdom toward those who are outside,
redeeming the time. Let your speech always
be with grace, seasoned with salt, that you may
know how you ought to answer each one.*

COLOSSIANS 4:5–6 NKJV

Lord and Savior, I'm so grateful that You've forgiven me, saved me, and made me a part of Your family of believers. Your Word tells me that I am always to be prepared to share Your message of salvation with people in my sphere of influence. But I have to admit that I don't always know what to say or how to say it. Colossians 4:5–6 suggests that I should tell Your truth in a way that best connects with those I know need You. May my speech reflect my passion and love for Your message. And please remind me daily why Your Gospel is such an amazing message.

AN EFFECTIVE TEACHER

For I have given you an example,
that ye should do as I have done to you.
JOHN 13:15 KJV

★ ★ ★

Heavenly Father, I appreciate reading about the life of Your Son and seeing how He taught the world about Your love through His example and teachings. He portrayed compassion by healing the sick and feeding the multitudes. He expressed the depth of Your forgiveness by giving His life for my sins. Lord, help me communicate Your teachings by my example as I live out my life of faith in front of other people.

BEARING FRUIT

*But the fruit of the Spirit is love, joy, peace,
longsuffering, kindness, goodness, faithfulness,
gentleness, self-control. Against such there is no law.*
GALATIANS 5:22–23 NKJV

Father in heaven, You call me as a Christian man to
live life with certain character qualities. I confess that
I fall short in many of those areas. I'm not always as
loving as I should be, and I'm not always patient. But I
know You've given me a way to project Your love, joy,
patience, kindness, and other qualities—You've placed
Your Holy Spirit inside me, and He helps me to bear the
fruits You've listed in Your Word. Thank You, Lord, for
Your Holy Spirit. Thank You that His work causes me
to be the kind of man You've called me to be.

DREADFUL SUPERSTITION

Regard not them that have familiar spirits,
neither seek after wizards, to be defiled
by them: I am the LORD your God.

LEVITICUS 19:31 KJV

Father, help me guard against falling into superstition under its many guises. I unfold and read a slip of paper with my fortune from a Chinese cookie, but I place no credence upon anything it says. I open the entertainment section of the newspaper and see the horoscopes for that day, but I push such nonsense out of my mind and turn the page. Father, help me continue to ignore and avoid these and all other dreadful superstitions. My trust is not in fortune-telling but in You and Your Word.

TRUST IN HIS RIGHTEOUSNESS

In thee, O LORD, do I put my trust; let me never be ashamed: deliver me in thy righteousness.

PSALM 31:1 KJV

★ ★ ★

Heavenly Father, I look at a photo of myself taken years ago and marvel at how much I have changed. The greatest change has been on the inside. Righteous Lord, before I made a commitment to You, I tried to run my own life. I ignored the advice of friends and became angry over their concern for me. My emotions were out of control. Today, I wonder how anyone managed to tolerate me. Thank You, Lord, for delivering me from my former self. No longer do I feel I must be a self-made man. I experience peace in knowing You as my Savior. I trust You to be my guide.

IT'S WHAT'S IN THE HEART

*"You have heard that it was said to those of old,
'You shall not commit adultery.' But I say to you
that whoever looks at a woman to lust for her has
already committed adultery with her in his heart."*

MATTHEW 5:27–28 NKJV

God of holiness, I can find myself falling into the trap
of thinking that it's okay to consider sexual sin as long
as I don't commit "the act." But You've warned me
that allowing my heart and mind to go where I know
my body shouldn't is as bad in Your eyes as actually
doing the deed. Lord, it's so hard to control my
thoughts. But I know that with Your help, I can do anything. Please train my mind to dwell on You and not
on things I know displease You.

A PART TO PLAY

*And He gave some as apostles, and
some as prophets, and some as evangelists,
and some as pastors and teachers, for the
equipping of the saints for the work of service,
to the building up of the body of Christ.*

EPHESIANS 4:11–12 NASB

Lord Jesus, You didn't save me just so I could go to church and just sit there every Sunday, doing nothing of benefit to my brothers and sisters in faith. You've given me gifts and abilities so I can serve, so I can make a difference in my congregation and in the world around me. Here I am, Lord. I want to be an instrument in Your hand. Move me and enable me to serve in the way that benefits others and glorifies You.

VICTORY OVER THE GIANT

*David said moreover, The LORD that delivered
me out of the paw of the lion, and out of the
paw of the bear, he will deliver me out
of the hand of this Philistine.*

1 SAMUEL 17:37 KJV

Dear God, I work out in a gym, but despite my efforts,
I will probably never be as strong as some of the men
there who lift weights. Mighty Lord, I am happy that
You do not require physical strength to do battle
for righteousness. You helped young David defeat
Goliath with just one stone and a sling because he
trusted You to be his deliverer. Likewise, I offer You
my faith with the understanding that You will make
it powerful enough to conquer situations regardless
of how hopeless they may seem.

SELF-HELP

*The word of the Lord endureth for
ever. And this is the word which
by the gospel is preached unto you.*
1 PETER 1:25 KJV

Father, around the office I see people carrying self-help books to read during their lunch breaks. Each month another title makes the best-seller list. Yet, few have enough substance to be enduring classics. Lord, when I study my human nature, I find many constants in my character—I am sinful, selfish, full of pride, sometimes afraid, and always facing death. The Bible addresses all these issues. Your Word is more thorough than any contemporary book that would try to show me how to improve myself without Your assistance. May I always remember to turn to Your enduring guidebook for daily living and eternal salvation.

REMEMBERING

Then I thought, "To this I will appeal: the years when the Most High stretched out his right hand. I will remember the deeds of the LORD; yes, I will remember your miracles of long ago."

PSALM 77:10–11 NIV

Mighty God, You've done so many great things—even miraculous things—for me since I came to know You. I recognize that You want me to remember those things and to share them with others so that they too can see Your compassion and greatness. Thank You for giving me examples of Your amazing deeds—both in the lives of people in Your word and in my own life and the lives of those close to me. Remind me of these things every day, especially when You give me an opportunity to talk to others about You.

YOU CAN'T TAKE IT WITH YOU

*Don't wear yourself out trying to get rich;
restrain yourself! Riches disappear in the
blink of an eye; wealth sprouts wings and
flies off into the wild blue yonder.*

PROVERBS 23:4–5 MSG

Father God, Your Word warns me over and over that I
am not to love money or possessions, that I am to see
them simply as a tool to serve You and other people.
Yet the lure of worldly riches sometimes still clamors
for my attention. Lord, forgive me if even the smallest part of me loves money. Remind me daily that my
money and things won't follow me into eternity. Help
me to trust You in my work life and finances, and
help me to glorify You through them in every way.

MOVING OUT IN FAITH

The official pleaded, "Lord, please come now before my little boy dies." Then Jesus told him, "Go back home. Your son will live!" And the man believed what Jesus said and started home.

JOHN 4:49–50 NLT

★ ★ ★

Precious Jesus, thank You for Your willingness to respond when I call out to You in my times of need. Lord, in the past, I've simply asked You to show up during those times, and You've asked me to step out, believing that my prayer has been answered. Help me to be willing to go to additional lengths to seek You when You tell me to do just that.

★ AN ANTIDOTE TO WORRY ★

Do not be anxious about anything, but in every situation, by prayer and petition, with thanksgiving, present your requests to God. And the peace of God, which transcends all understanding, will guard your hearts and your minds in Christ Jesus.

PHILIPPIANS 4:6–7 NIV

★   ★   ★

My precious Lord, I confess that I'm sometimes given to worry. I worry about things most men feel anxious about these days, but I know it's not Your will that I lose sleep and get my guts in a knot over things I can't control. You want me to live in the peace that comes from knowing that You are in control and that You care for me and the people I love. May I always come to You first when I face a situation that causes me to worry.

Day 220

★ CONTROLLING YOUR TONGUE ★

*Those who consider themselves religious and yet
do not keep a tight rein on their tongues deceive
themselves, and their religion is worthless.*

JAMES 1:26 NIV

Lord God, I sometimes cringe when I read James 1:26. I confess that I occasionally say things that I know don't please You—things that don't encourage or build up others. On my own, it seems that I can't control my tongue any more than I can keep my mind pure or my actions blameless. Forgive me for saying things I shouldn't. Help me to speak only words that glorify You and benefit my brothers and sisters in Christ. And when I don't have something good to say, Father, please give me Your good words!

CROWN OF LIFE

*I have fought a good fight, I have finished my
course, I have kept the faith: henceforth there
is laid up for me a crown of righteousness.*
2 TIMOTHY 4:7–8 KJV

Father, as I watch television broadcasts of British
royalty wearing their jeweled crowns, I cannot help
but be impressed with the pomp and ceremony sur-
rounding their public appearances. However, I know
that they have lives as brief as mine. They will die,
leaving behind their riches.

Father, help me focus on the One who wore the
crown of thorns. That terrible crown is gone now,
but Jesus is still alive. I look forward to wearing the
crown of eternal life. Dear Lord, I can never earn
that priceless gift. You freely give it to me and all who
have been faithful.

BLESS MY DEEDS

But whoso looketh into the perfect law of liberty, and continueth therein, he being not a forgetful hearer, but a doer of the work, this man shall be blessed in his deed.

JAMES 1:25 KJV

Father, I like to play football from the comfort of my living room. From my safe haven on the couch, I yell at players for making mistakes and criticize the coach's decisions. A crossing pattern here, a quarterback sneak there.

If I were a coach, what magnificent plays I would call! Lord, in church projects I often contribute more advice than work. It is so much easier to tell a person what needs to be done than to actually do it. Help me to get involved in church business. Give me a spirit of unity and a positive attitude in working with others to build up Your kingdom. Thank You for promising to bless my deeds.

═══ A MATTER OF TRUST ═══

*"Therefore I say to you, do not worry about your life,
what you will eat or what you will drink; nor about
your body, what you will put on. . . . Look at the birds
of the air, for they neither sow nor reap nor gather
into barns; yet your heavenly Father feeds them.
Are you not of more value than they?"*

MATTHEW 6:25–26 NKJV

My Father and provider, I confess that I often worry
about how I'm going to care for myself and my family.
How will I be able to pay for the things we'll need in
the future? Lord, please forgive me for my lack of trust
in You. You care about our needs even more than I do.
You have promised to provide for us, so help me to
rest in the fact that You always keep Your promises.

GOD AS MY SHEPHERD

*Know that the LORD, He is God; it is He
who has made us, and [a]not we ourselves;
we are His people and the sheep of His pasture.*
PSALM 100:3 NKJV

Protector God, thank You for being a shepherd to
me. A good shepherd protects and provides for his
sheep and guides them to the best places to eat and
rest. Then they can have the energy it takes to do
the things sheep do every day. But You aren't just a
good shepherd, You are the *perfect* shepherd. Lord,
You provide me all I need each day, starting with Your
love and protection. You restore me when I feel worn
down, and You would never lead me anywhere but to
a place of righteousness. Thank You, not just for what
You do for me, but also for who You are.

PREJUDICE

Thou shalt not avenge, nor bear any grudge
against the children of thy people, but thou shalt
love thy neighbour as thyself: I am the LORD.
LEVITICUS 19:18 KJV

★ ★ ★

Jesus, You have taught me that to live in heaven forever with You, I must be a good neighbor. Your parable about the Samaritan who offered aid shows that every person should be treated with kindness, even people that others might hate or despise because of their language, skin color, or place of birth. Lord, so that I can live with You in heaven, give me the determination to act upon the truth that all people are equal in Your sight. Let me show kindness to everyone, because all are created in Your image.

★ A CHRISTIAN GENTLEMAN ★

Who shall ascend into the hill of the LORD? or who shall stand in his holy place? He that hath clean hands, and a pure heart; who hath not lifted up his soul unto vanity, nor sworn deceitfully.

PSALM 24:3–4 KJV

Father, why do I think of a bride in a white dress as a symbol of purity? Purity is not a term that readily comes to my mind as a male attribute. But I know that sexual morality, temperance, chastity, and purity are characteristics that I should strive to achieve. In another age, a man who strove for a well-mannered life would be described as a Christian gentleman. I would be happy to wear that title, and I would take it as a compliment. I pray that I will be naturally courteous, live with dignity, and willingly follow a high standard of conduct. If the execution of my intentions falls short, may the purity of my intentions be obvious. May I live up to what You expect of me.

═══ GUARD YOUR HEART ═══

*"But take heed to yourselves, lest your
hearts be weighed down with carousing,
drunkenness, and cares of this life,
and that Day come on you unexpectedly."*

LUKE 21:34 NKJV

Gracious Father, many things in this world have the potential to weigh down my heart and cause me to stray from You. If it's not the daily temptations to sin, it's the legitimate cares and concerns that life on earth presents. I know You want me to follow You and serve You with an undivided heart—and that's what I want too. You've saved me and made me a part of Your family, so help me to show my gratitude by fervently guarding the new heart You've placed within me. Keep me focused on You first, and help me to handle the things that could come between us.

MORE LIKE YOU

That they all may be one; as thou, Father, art in me, and I in thee, that they also may be one in us: that the world may believe that thou hast sent me.

JOHN 17:21 KJV

Father, when I see an elderly couple that has spent a lifetime together in love, I find it remarkable how they anticipate one another's needs, how they communicate with merely a nod or a gesture, and, in some cases, how they have developed similar physical characteristics. Father, I pray that during my life, I can in the same way become one with You. I want to absorb Your Word so thoroughly that I know Your will because it has become a part of me. I pray that I can talk with You easily and often because it has become my nature. And most of all, I pray that I will have the same spiritual characteristics as You.

A GOOD STEWARD

*And let us consider one another to
provoke unto love and to good works.*
HEBREWS 10:24 KJV

Gracious Lord, when I consider Your abundant blessings, I take seriously my responsibility to be a good steward. I dedicate to Your work the assets—both tangible and intangible—You have temporarily given to my trust. I pray that the manner in which I share my blessings with others will be a beacon that proclaims Your love. I know that the only treasures safe from ruin are those I have surrendered to You. When the time comes for me to stand before You, I pray that I will be found a trustworthy steward.

Day 230

DOING GOOD FOR OTHERS

Let us not become weary in doing good,
for at the proper time we will reap a harvest
if we do not give up. Therefore, as we have
opportunity, let us do good to all people, especially
to those who belong to the family of believers.
GALATIANS 6:9–10 NIV

Compassionate God, You've done so much good for me, starting with bringing me into Your family of believers. You love every member of Your family, and You call us to love one another in word and in deed. Lord, I confess that giving of myself to others, especially those in my spiritual family, can sometimes be draining. Please fill my heart with a desire to selflessly serve others, then give me opportunities to do just that. I love You and want to honor You by taking advantage of every opportunity to serve.

═══ SPIRITUAL POVERTY ═══

*But grow in grace, and in the knowledge
of our Lord and Saviour Jesus Christ. To him
be glory both now and for ever. Amen.*
2 PETER 3:18 KJV

★ ★ ★

Father, I am struck by the fact that, despite living in a wealthy nation, citizens with an inferior education may live as if they were in an underdeveloped country. Often I fail to understand that this principle applies to my spiritual life as well. Lord, I am blessed with so many ways to delve deeply into Your Word. The Bible is available in both paper and electronic form. Bible dictionaries and other aids for studying Scripture abound in many editions. Dedicated teachers conduct Bible studies tailored to the level of my understanding. I pray, dear Father, that I will take advantage of the opportunities to have a world-class spiritual education so that I will escape the poverty of spiritual ignorance.

═══ GIVING OF WHAT YOU HAVE ═══

[Jesus] also saw a poor widow put in two very small copper coins. "Truly I tell you," he said, "this poor widow has put in more than all the others. All these people gave their gifts out of their wealth; but she out of her poverty put in all she had to live on."

LUKE 21:2–4 NIV

Father in heaven, I know You want me to be a generous man. But sometimes, because my bank account is so depleted, I find myself afraid to give to Your work here on earth. I confess that my fear often comes from not fully trusting You to care for me when I give from what You've given me. So make me courageous and faithful to give of what I have, knowing that it blesses others—and leads to blessings for me and my family.

THE END

For God so loved the world, that he gave his only begotten Son, that whosoever believeth in him should not perish, but have everlasting life.
JOHN 3:16 KJV

Father, I avoid reading movie or book reviews that go into too much detail about the plot. I enjoy the suspense of waiting to learn how the story unfolds. The ending may be happy or it may have a twist, but I want to be surprised by it.

However, in my own life I want to know the final result. Thank You, Lord, for telling me the outcome. You have promised that if I seek You, I will find You. Jesus has already paid the penalty for my sins. A faithful life assures me that I will have an eternal home with You.

INTELLECTUAL APPEAL

*The simple believeth every word: but the
prudent man looketh well to his going.*
PROVERBS 14:15 KJV

Lord, every day my eyes and ears are assailed by those who want to bend my will to their purposes. Testimonies from famous personalities, glittering television advertisements, and half-truths of insincere politicians are all trying to muddle my reasoning so I cannot distinguish between truth and lies. They want me to listen and not ask questions.

Father, help me use the abilities You have given me to carefully evaluate the claims of those who try to influence me. I appreciate that You appeal to my intellect as well as my emotions. You tell me to work out my own salvation and try the spirits to see if they are from You. Give me discernment in spiritual and everyday matters.

SERVING ABOVE REPROACH

We want to avoid any criticism of the way we administer this liberal gift. For we are taking pains to do what is right, not only in the eyes of the Lord but also in the eyes of man.

2 CORINTHIANS 8:20–21 NIV

God of righteousness, You tell me in Your written Word that I am to conform my thinking and behavior to the standards You've set for me, not to the world's standards. At the same time, You want me to examine my own behavior and motives to be sure I never invite scorn or criticism over the things I do for You. Lord, You've warned me that the world will oppose me because I serve You. May I never do anything to make it easier for people to criticize.

HAPPY IN THE LORD

Happy is that people, that is in such a case: yea,
happy is that people, whose God is the LORD.
PSALM 144:15 KJV

★ ★ ★

Lord, as I look up to heaven, I am overwhelmed with a spirit of happiness. I delight in knowing You as the Creator of this universe, who designed me to reflect Your character.

Lord, I consider it a benefit to be in Your lineage. I delight in having You as my heavenly Father. You give me strength to find victory in difficult situations. In easy times or in difficult ones, I know that I benefit from my walk with You. Regardless of the circumstances, may my disposition be one that recognizes the everlasting happiness I have in knowing You.

═══ **THE PICTURE JESUS SEES** ═══

*According as he hath chosen us in him before
the foundation of the world, that we should be
holy and without blame before him in love.*

EPHESIANS 1:4 KJV

Dear Lord, with an auto-everything digital camera, even I can take pictures. But I have found that snapping the shutter does not guarantee a good photo. I've learned to aim the camera to cut out distracting elements such as road signs, to avoid trees growing out of heads, and to keep power lines from cutting across a scenic view. Sometimes I have to use a flash to illuminate a dark subject.

Jesus, in Your honored position of viewing earth from heaven, what image of my life do You see? Remove all distracting elements from my Christian character. Illuminate me with Your love, and frame me in Your Word. I pray You will compose my life so it presents a pleasing picture to others—and to You.

FINDING STRENGTH IN. . .WEAKNESS?

But he said to me, "My grace is sufficient for you, for my power is made perfect in weakness." Therefore I will boast all the more gladly about my weaknesses, so that Christ's power may rest on me.

2 CORINTHIANS 12:9 NIV

Mighty God, You know how we men think. You know that we esteem physical and mental strength above most everything, and You know that the last thing we want to admit to is weakness of any kind. But Your Word tells me that when I acknowledge my weaknesses, You have me right where You want me. You want to empower me to do great things for You, but You also want me to acknowledge that without You, I am not just weak—I'm powerless. So, Lord, I embrace the fact that without You, I can't do anything.

★ ON AUTOPILOT ★

Learn to do well; seek judgment,
relieve the oppressed, judge the
fatherless, plead for the widow.
ISAIAH 1:17 KJV

Lord, I was driving when I realized with a start that I'd passed my turn. I'd taken the same route to work so often that on the weekend, when my destination was in the same direction, I'd continued on as if going to work. I was on autopilot, not thinking of my purpose or where I was going.

Father, in my spiritual life, I sometimes go on autopilot. I unconsciously let religious ceremonies and thoughtless worship substitute for honest and meaningful living. Serving You can cause weariness for me and those around me when it becomes a ritual. Help me develop enthusiasm and delight for a conscious Christian walk.

UNDERSTANDING THE TIMES

*Of the sons of Issachar, men who understood
the times, with knowledge of what Israel
should do, their chiefs were two hundred;
and all their kinsmen were at their command.*

1 CHRONICLES 12:32 NASB

Sovereign God, some days I'm confused and more
than a little bewildered. I look around and see a world
that is drifting further and further away from You and
Your standards. It seems like many of our churches
are quickly coming to a point where they no longer
honor You as they should and no longer preach and
teach the truth of Your Word. I'm not even sure how I
should pray about these things, let alone what I should
do. Please, give me wisdom and understanding so I
can know how to respond.

HOPE

*And Joshua said unto them, Fear not,
nor be dismayed, be strong and of good
courage: for thus shall the LORD do to all
your enemies against whom ye fight.*

JOSHUA 10:25 KJV

Father, sometimes I become despondent. My outlook becomes gloomy. It is as if some of the light has gone out in my life. Yet, such a feeling would only be justified if I were without hope, and that is certainly not the case. Your love, the grace of Jesus Christ, and the guidance of the Holy Spirit are with me.

Father, help me face the challenges before me with boldness. Give me strength to shake off anything that troubles my mind so that I can press on each day with a clear purpose. Help me ignore any troubling concerns that might slow my steps.

Day 242

RIGHTEOUS PERSUASION

*When the righteous are in authority,
the people rejoice: but when the wicked
beareth rule, the people mourn.*
PROVERBS 29:2 KJV

Guide me, Lord, when I am responsible for launching an activity that requires the participation of others. Help me to exercise energy and enthusiasm in enlisting their participation. May I study and test ideas so I will be respected as a source of advice. I do not want a discussion to be a contest I must win but rather a validation that I am applying Christian principles to the issue. Remind me that I can be right and yet be ineffective if I fail to act out of love. Allow my tone, temper, and manner to flow from my devotion to Your truth.

AN AGREEMENT WITH YOUR EYES

*"I made a covenant with my eyes
not to look lustfully at a young woman."*
JOB 31:1 NIV

My loving Father in heaven, in this world it's not easy to keep my eyes from seeing things that can cause impure thoughts. I could stop watching television and going to movies, and I could completely cut myself off from the internet, and I'd still be bombarded daily with sexual, sensual images. The only way I could completely avoid these things would be to lock myself in a room with no media access—or join a monastery. I don't think You want either of these options for me. But, like Job, I can start by making an agreement with You—and with my eyes—that I won't intentionally look at anything that could stir up sinful thoughts.

WALKING WITH GOD

Noah was a just man and perfect in his generations, and Noah walked with God.
GENESIS 6:9 KJV

★ ★ ★

Lord, I am defined by whom I choose as my heroes and whom I pattern my life after. Others interpret my character by those with whom I walk. I want to be like the heroes of old, those men of renown in the Old Testament, who were described as having "walked with God."

Dear Father, give me the determination to walk at Your side. I seek an honorable walk that shows Your power and character. I know that I am not walking alone; You are with me. I have victory over impossible circumstances because I have placed myself in Your footsteps.

A SONG OF PRAISE

The LORD is my strength and my shield; my heart trusted in him, and I am helped: therefore my heart greatly rejoiceth; and with my song will I praise him.

PSALM 28:7 KJV

I sing to You, O Lord, a continual song of praise. I declare Your name to all those who come into my presence. Words of thanksgiving are forever upon my lips. I can sing a new song because of Your grace and power.

Your holy name is exalted in heaven and on earth, O Lord Most High. Your righteousness causes my heart to rejoice and break forth in a song of praise: "Glory to the God of my salvation. The generosity of Your compassion overwhelms my soul."

⸻ INTERNAL CONFLICT ⸻

So I say, walk by the Spirit, and you will not gratify the desires of the flesh. For the flesh desires what is contrary to the Spirit, and the Spirit what is contrary to the flesh. They are in conflict with each other, so that you are not to do whatever you want.

GALATIANS 5:16–17 NIV

God of power, I thank You for Your Holy Spirit, who teaches me, encourages me, and empowers me as I battle with my own fleshly desires. I have a war raging inside me, Lord, and when I try to overcome temptation through my own human willpower, I fail every time. But when I rely on Your Holy Spirit, I have victory over my sinful desires. Thank You for making a way for me to live the way You want me to live.

FOR BOLDNESS

And in nothing terrified by your adversaries:
which is to them an evident token of perdition,
but to you of salvation, and that of God.
PHILIPPIANS 1:28 KJV

★ ★ ★

Dear Lord, each day I encounter people who have chosen to walk a path that conflicts with Your laws and those of our government. Their goals are contrary to honest living, and they identify me as their adversary. I pray for fearlessness born of confidence in Your protection as I confront evil.

Father, You give me boldness greater than my natural ability. I walk by Your side, and with Your strength I overcome the fear of what others might do to me. Help me develop strength of spirit, physical courage, and the intelligence to rightly employ them when they are required.

SYNCHRONIZE

*And God said, Let there be lights in the
firmament of the heaven to divide the
day from the night; and let them be for signs,
and for seasons, and for days, and years.*
GENESIS 1:14 KJV

I've stopped wearing a watch, Lord, not because time
is no longer important to me, but because everywhere I go, clocks, watches, and electronic gadgets
constantly show the time. My phone, microwave, car
radio, and computer screen display the time. The time
is everywhere!

Lord, You created time and gave us the dependable progression of the sun, moon, and stars to mark
off days, seasons, and years. Help me recognize each
moment as a gift from You. I pray that I will plan my
day to be in sync with Your eternal purposes.

A TO-DO LIST CHRISTIAN

To every thing there is a season, and a
time to every purpose under the heaven.
ECCLESIASTES 3:1 KJV

I am a to-do list person, Lord. The multitude of those activities threaten to spill into the time I have set aside for prayer. I've moved prayer to category one—an absolutely, positively, must-do activity. Forgive me when taking time to talk to You does not come automatically and naturally.

Father, You'll notice the pad of paper at my side as I come to You in prayer. When unfinished items intrude on my mind, I'll write them down and set them aside so that I can concentrate on talking with You. I am thankful that we have this time to spend together.

BUILDING UP THE BODY OF CHRIST

We urge you, brethren, admonish the unruly, encourage the fainthearted, help the weak, be patient with everyone. See that no one repays another with evil for evil, but always seek after that which is good for one another and for all people.

1 THESSALONIANS 5:14–15 NASB

Lord God, You've given me the ability (and the responsibility) to help others along in their life of faith in You. And the things You've given me to do in 1 Thessalonians 5 don't require me to have any special training or education—just a willingness to reach out to my brothers who need it. Give me the courage to challenge, encourage, and help out when it's needed. Above all, give me the patience I need to deal with people who are as imperfect as I am.

★ A RESOLUTE HEART ★

*But Daniel purposed in his heart that he would
not defile himself with the portion of the king's
meat, nor with the wine which he drank:
therefore he requested of the prince of the
eunuchs that he might not defile himself.*
DANIEL 1:8 KJV

★ ★ ★

Heavenly Father, despite the quiet time I am experiencing now, I know that challenges will test me—if not later today, then sometime soon. Once temptations are upon me, there is seldom adequate time or the proper environment to make a reasoned response. My goal is to look ahead, consider the evils I may face, and make the right decision before the events occur.

Even so, Lord, after I make an important decision, there is a time of second-guessing, both from myself and from others. Rid my mind of doubts that serve no useful end. I pray I will be resolute and boldly live a consistent, purposeful life.

REPAYING EVIL

Do not repay evil with evil or insult with insult. On the contrary, repay evil with blessing, because to this you were called so that you may inherit a blessing.

1 PETER 3:9 NIV

Merciful God, You know me well enough to realize it's not easy for me to hold my tongue and keep from retaliating when someone speaks ill of me. But I know You well enough that I understand that this is not how I should respond when someone does or says something to insult me. On my own, I can't bless someone who does me wrong. So make me more like Jesus, who endured horrific insults and abuse, doing nothing but *bless* those who truly deserved Your retribution.

★ A GOOD REPUTATION ★

Moreover he must have a good report of them which are without; lest he fall into reproach and the snare of the devil.
1 TIMOTHY 3:7 KJV

Father, I carry two names—my own and "Christian." Help me develop a good reputation that brings honor to You and other Christians. Only You can soften my character and reset it in the mold You desire. Although I cannot live a perfect life, Lord, help me to have a good reputation by following the guidelines set forth in the Bible.

Lord, I cannot help but be aware that it is difficult to recover a good reputation once it has been tarnished. Please help me keep Your presence in my life, and deliver me from the evil forces that would destroy my name.

CHOICES

*That he would grant unto us, that we being
delivered out of the hand of our enemies
might serve him without fear, in holiness and
righteousness before him, all the days of our life.*
LUKE 1:74–75 KJV

Father, I have seen that accidents occur when a person tries to accomplish two tasks at the same time. Often, neither one is done well, and sometimes the balancing act of trying to achieve two different goals leads to disaster.

In Your Word I read about the impossibility of serving two masters. I commit to You my time, talent, money, and physical and emotional energy. I pray that I will be single-minded so that when a situation calls for action, I will not hesitate to serve You.

HEAVENLY PEACE

*"Peace I leave with you; my peace I give you.
I do not give to you as the world gives. Do not let
your hearts be troubled and do not be afraid."*

JOHN 14:27 NIV

Lord Jesus, sometimes it feels like my life is spinning out of control. Pressures at work, anxiety about my family, and other major concerns overwhelm me. I need some peace of mind, and I need it today. Nothing this world has to offer, not even the caring words of my best friends, helps. But You promised me peace, the kind of peace only You can give. Lord, calm my heart and ease my mind today as I bring all my worries and lay them at Your feet. And once I bring them to You, give me the faith it takes to leave them there and never pick them up again.

HONOR

And he said unto him, Behold now, there is in this city a man of God, and he is an honourable man; all that he saith cometh surely to pass: now let us go thither; peradventure he can shew us our way that we should go.

1 SAMUEL 9:6 KJV

Thank You, Lord, for the place of honor You give me in Your Kingdom. As armor helps keep a warrior safe in battle, You shield me from the fiery darts of evil. It is Your assistance that makes it possible for me to live an honorable life. I need Your protective covering to cast off the works of darkness.

Lord, help me live a consistent life so that those who don't know You will be drawn to You. I pray that I will have a good name in the community and that I will direct others to heaven.

KEEP YOUR COOL!

So then, my beloved brethren, let every man be swift to hear, slow to speak, slow to wrath; for the wrath of man does not produce the righteousness of God.
JAMES 1:19–20 NKJV

Father in heaven, I understand that anger itself isn't necessarily sinful, and I know that You call men to speak words of truth into a situation when they are needed. But I also know that if I'm not careful, I can easily become angry when I don't understand the whole story—and then say things I shouldn't. Please give me a listening ear. Help me to hold my tongue when I don't have anything positive to contribute. I know that my own anger doesn't produce the results You desire, so help me keep my emotions in check. I want to avoid sinful, damaging anger.

LIVING FAITH

What good is it, my brothers and sisters,
if someone claims to have faith but has no
deeds? Can such faith save them? . . . Faith by
itself, if it is not accompanied by action, is dead.

JAMES 2:14, 17 NIV

★ ★ ★

Lord Jesus, You've promised me in Your written Word that my salvation is a gift from You, granted when I put my faith in Your work on the cross. But You also told Your followers that knowing You would result in good works, all of which glorify You as other people see that this faith is real and living. Lord, show me what good works You'd like me to accomplish today. You've already saved and transformed me, so please show me and others that my faith is real, by the good I do in Your wonderful name.

PRAISE IN THE ASSEMBLY

To appoint unto them that mourn in Zion, to give unto them beauty for ashes, the oil of joy for mourning, the garment of praise for the spirit of heaviness. . .that he might be glorified.

ISAIAH 61:3 KJV

Thank You, Lord, that in Your wisdom You have given me Your day as a reminder to rest and renew. As I assemble with other believers, the stresses of the week dissipate. I feel Your living Spirit as the unified Body of Christ worships You.

I thank You, Lord, for allowing me to be a part of the assembly, where the cares of the week are put aside. There is joy in my heart as I leave Your house. Fellowship with other believers ignites a fire that burns in my heart throughout the week.

BEING A PRAYER WARRIOR

Epaphras, who is one of you and a servant of Christ Jesus, sends greetings. He is always wrestling in prayer for you, that you may stand firm in all the will of God, mature and fully assured.

Colossians 4:12 niv

Father, Epaphras isn't one of the better-known men in the Bible. But what's important isn't how well he's known, but what he's known for. Epaphras was a prayer warrior, and Your written Word honors him for that. Lord, I know You look for men willing spend time before You on behalf of others, and I want to be that kind of man. I want to be someone who says "I'll pray for you," and then follows through. More than that, though, I want You to see me as a man committed to coming to You every day in prayer for whatever You lay on my heart.

DYNAMIC LEADERSHIP

*Stand therefore, having your loins girt about
with truth, and having on the breastplate of
righteousness; and your feet shod with the
preparation of the gospel of peace.*

Ephesians 6:14–15 KJV

Father, when I am called upon to be a leader, I sometimes feel that I am not the one best equipped to lead. Grant me the capacity to confront this apprehension and overcome it. When making decisions, may I always listen to others so they will gladly participate in our common goal. Equip me to follow Your guidance and direction so that I select the right course of action.

I know that my leadership may not be universally accepted. Let me be unflinching in carrying out my work, despite criticism. May I lead by example and with a humble attitude.

FOOD FOR THOUGHT

*As newborn babes, desire the sincere milk
of the word, that ye may grow thereby.*
1 PETER 2:2 KJV

Dear Lord, as a new Christian, I read the Bible to gain spiritual maturity. Unlike my physical body, my spiritual maturity can continue to grow throughout my life. Yes, reading the Bible provides spiritual food for my soul. It helps me grow. But just as importantly, it repairs the damage done by living in a world where each day brings challenges to my Christian character.

O God, now that I am further along in my walk with You, I recognize that the world produces wear and tear on my spiritual body. It must be repaired and given fresh energy by daily renewal through Your Word.

TALENTS

*But now hath God set the members every one
of them in the body, as it hath pleased him.*

1 Corinthians 12:18 kjv

Heavenly Father, when I listen to heartfelt singing at church, glory from heaven seems to be radiating from each singer's lips. Even my off-key notes do not distract from our praises.

When it comes to singing, I admire the talents of others and realize how limited I am. But, Lord, in Your Word I read how You give each person a different capacity. You have designed me to be a unique individual. My talents may seem less significant than those of others, but I want to use the abilities that I do have for Your glory.

WHEN GOD IS SILENT

*How long, LORD, must I call for help,
but you do not listen? Or cry out to you,
"Violence!" but you do not save?*
HABAKKUK 1:2 NIV

Faithful God, there have been times in my walk with You when I've prayed fervently, consistently, and persistently over some important issue, but I felt like You weren't hearing me. In times like that, please give me the assurance that You haven't forgotten me—that You are still concerned over the issues that cause me to lose sleep. Help me to remember Your promise to hear my prayers when I call out to You. Lord, I don't know why You sometimes wait before You answer, but when You delay, please help me to continue trusting You.

DELIGHT

*And not only so, but we also joy in God
through our Lord Jesus Christ, by whom
we have now received the atonement.*
ROMANS 5:11 KJV

All joy comes from You, Lord. I can experience joy because of the risen Christ. I no longer have the heavy weight of my transgressions to discourage me. Your joy lifts my spirit and relieves my anxieties. Thank You, Lord, for joy that gives me strength to run this spiritual race.

Lord, for my joy to be fully realized, I must share it with others. My desire is to let joy, a fruit of the Spirit, flourish in my life. Help me bless others by allowing You to shine on them through my life.

Day 266

FOR GOVERNMENT LEADERS

*I exhort therefore, that, first of all, supplications,
prayers, intercessions, and giving of thanks,
be made for all men; for kings, and for all that
are in authority; that we may lead a quiet and
peaceable life in all godliness and honesty.*
1 TIMOTHY 2:1–2 KJV

Heavenly Father, I ask that You guide the leaders of my country. May they have integrity, morality, and leadership ability. Guide them to extend Your influence into all areas of society. Empower them to overcome the dark forces at work in the world.

Father, I ask for Your guidance upon my government's leaders. Direct them to take our nation in the way You would have us go. Help them realize that true prosperity comes only through the application of Christian values. May the laws they make uphold and protect our right to worship You.

EMERGENCY WORKERS

Defend the poor and fatherless:
do justice to the afflicted and needy.
PSALM 82:3 KJV

Almighty God, I pray for those who respond to emergencies, whether police, firefighters, or medical personnel. Please protect these public servants as they come to the rescue of those in dangerous situations. Provide them with the courage and wisdom to extricate others and themselves from the scenes of crisis.

Guide our police as they make split-second decisions in emotionally charged situations. Watch over our firefighters as their jobs take them into harm's way. Give our medical personnel skillful hands and clear minds as they rush to save lives. Grant all of these individuals the ability to act quickly and compassionately.

FREE TO SERVE

You, my brothers and sisters, were called to be free. But do not use your freedom to indulge the flesh; rather, serve one another humbly in love. For the entire law is fulfilled in keeping this one command: "Love your neighbor as yourself."

GALATIANS 5:13–14 NIV

Thank You, Jesus, for coming to earth to live and die and rise from the dead so that I could be freed from the terrible prison of sin. Keep me from walking back into that kind of bondage. I want to use my freedom to serve You and other people—not out of some need to atone for my own wrongdoing but out of pure, humble, godly love. I'm free, so now I can move my focus away from myself and onto loving You and others. Thank You for freeing me.

YOUTH AND VIGOR

*Lo, I am this day fourscore and five years old.
As yet I am as strong this day as I was in the
day that Moses sent me: as my strength
was then, even so is my strength now.*

JOSHUA 14:10–11 KJV

★ ★ ★

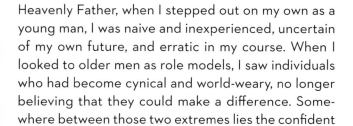

Heavenly Father, when I stepped out on my own as a young man, I was naive and inexperienced, uncertain of my own future, and erratic in my course. When I looked to older men as role models, I saw individuals who had become cynical and world-weary, no longer believing that they could make a difference. Somewhere between those two extremes lies the confident and vigorous man I want to be.

Dear Lord, give me an enthusiastic and vigorous mind, regardless of my age. Help me to renew and refresh myself by reading about the men of the Bible, those men of renown, who continued to follow You with youthful vigor despite their advancing years.

CONFRONTATION

But when Peter came to Antioch, I had to oppose him to his face, for what he did was very wrong.
GALATIANS 2:11 NLT

Gracious God, confronting a friend or brother in the Lord—even one who desperately needs it—is one of the toughest things You call a Christian man to do. It's probably safe to say that no one likes being confronted, and few enjoy doing the confronting. When I recognize that a friend or brother needs someone to step up and speak some words of correction, help me to first examine my own heart so I can know if *I* need to make any changes in my own attitudes and actions. Help me to choose my words carefully so that I don't come off as harsh or judgmental. Above all, may my motivation be one of pure love and genuine concern.

WITHSTANDING TRIALS

Blessed is the one who perseveres under trial because, having stood the test, that person will receive the crown of life that the Lord has promised to those who love him.

JAMES 1:12 NIV

Lord Jesus, You never promised Your followers an easy life, only that You would always be with them—even after You returned to heaven. Your Word tells me that trials and temptations will be a part of this life, and my own experiences confirm that truth. I'm encouraged and strengthened when I read that You have a crown of life waiting for me because I've endured every trial this world throws my way. Thank You for strengthening and encouraging me today and every day so that I don't just endure but prosper and grow as I overcome the trials I face.

COUNTING BLESSINGS

Enter into his gates with thanksgiving,
and into his courts with praise: be thankful
unto him, and bless his name.
PSALM 100:4 KJV

Dear Lord, what bountiful harvest I have received from You! I count blessings without number. You have given me health, a warm family life, prosperity, and a peaceful heart. You have given me strength in adversity and security in turmoil. You have given me opportunities to serve and thereby enriched my life.

I acknowledge the rich blessings that You have showered upon me. Help me appreciate them. Remove from my heart the idea that my recognition of these blessings will earn me future blessings. Let me focus on what You have done for me and rejoice in all the daily blessings You give me.

THE POWER OF WORDS

Let no corrupt word proceed out of your mouth,
but what is good for necessary edification,
that it may impart grace to the hearers.
EPHESIANS 4:29 NKJV

Loving heavenly Father, I confess that I'm not always careful with the words I speak. I sometimes say things I shouldn't, words that could hurt other people and damage their reputations. And I don't speak nearly enough words of encouragement and edification. I know that needs to change today. Lord, please check me when I'm about to say something I shouldn't. Not only that, but please give me words that build up and encourage others. Help me to replace my negative, hurtful speech with words that bless, encourage, and challenge others. Let every word that comes out of my mouth be helpful.

ENCOURAGING THOSE WHO SERVE

*But charge Joshua, and encourage him,
and strengthen him: for he shall go over
before this people, and he shall cause them
to inherit the land which thou shalt see.*

DEUTERONOMY 3:28 KJV

Lord, just as You instructed Moses to encourage Joshua to lead Your people across the Jordan River to enter the Promised Land, help me encourage those who have been chosen to serve. Help me ease their burdens and give them the will to continue the work You have called them to do.

When I am leading others, may I always be mindful of my role as Your servant. Help me choose the right words and actions to revitalize others when they have grown weary, assure them when they have doubts, console them in times of apparent failure, and reward them with heartfelt praise for their successes.

ATTITUDE

Create in me a clean heart, O God;
and renew a right spirit within me.
PSALM 51:10 KJV

★　★　★

Father, I am quick to focus on those things that affect me most directly. Often, I confess, I improperly view my wants as essentials. From minor matters such as restaurant service to more important ones such as making major purchases, I insist that my so-called requirements be fully met. I think and act as if those serving me should put my needs first.

Lord, keep a check on my attitude. I want to have a friendly disposition when I deal with others. Create in me a calm, controlled temperament. Help me have a "can do," "everything's okay" attitude rather than a "me" attitude.

Day 276

WHICH MASTER DO YOU SERVE?

"No one can serve two masters. Either you will hate the one and love the other, or you will be devoted to the one and despise the other. You cannot serve both God and money."

MATTHEW 6:24 NIV

Loving God, this world throws distractions at me daily—things that can turn into idols if I'm not careful. One of those distractions is money, which can be either a tool I use to serve You or an object of my affections. Lord, forgive me for putting money too high on my list of priorities. You know I need to earn money so I can care for my family, but help me to put money in its proper place. Remind me that it is simply a tool to help me do things You want me to do. . .it cannot be my life's focus.

PROPERLY MOTIVATED

"Take heed that you do not do your charitable deeds before men, to be seen by them. Otherwise you have no reward from your Father in heaven. Therefore, when you do a charitable deed, do not sound a trumpet before you as the hypocrites do in the synagogues and in the streets, that they may have glory from men. Assuredly, I say to you, they have their reward."

MATTHEW 6:1–2 NKJV

Lord Jesus, I know it's possible for me to do the right things for the wrong reasons. During Your earthly ministry, You taught Your followers to make certain that they never performed their good deeds or acts of charity in a way that brought attention to themselves. Remind me often to check my own heart to make sure that as I do good for others, my thoughts are of You first and of the person who benefits second.

NO FREE LUNCH

For by grace are ye saved through faith;
and that not of yourselves: it is the gift of God:
not of works, lest any man should boast.
EPHESIANS 2:8–9 KJV

Lord, because I have heard the statement "There is no such thing as a free lunch" so often, I view with skepticism anything that is offered for free. Even accepting Your grace is difficult. But You have overcome my reluctance by showing that although grace is free to me, it did come at a price. If I do not accept Your grace, then Jesus' death for me was in vain.

Father, I have become a privileged child, receiving favors and divine protection merely by accepting Your gift of salvation. You have delivered me from the captivity of sin and restored me to a life of freedom. Thank You, Lord.

═══ **VALUABLE TRIALS** ═══

*Consider it pure joy, my brothers and
sisters, whenever you face trials of many
kinds, because you know that the testing
of your faith produces perseverance. Let
perseverance finish its work so that you may
be mature and complete, not lacking anything.*
JAMES 1:2–4 NIV

★　★　★

Loving Father, when life throws difficulties my way,
feeling joyful goes against everything inside me. But
Your Word teaches me that You use all things for my
good and Your glory—and that includes the rotten
things that happen. Please make me humble, and give
me the understanding of just how much tough times
can help me grow into what You want me to be. When
I feel like complaining, please remind me that there is
great joy in the easy times. . .and even greater value
in the difficulties.

PRAYER OF PRAISE

His glory covered the heavens,
and the earth was full of his praise.

HABAKKUK 3:3 KJV

Almighty Father of all creation, accept this prayer of praise. I respect You, venerate You, and honor You as the Creator of the universe and everything in it. I recognize You as my Maker. I am thankful that You were too kind to create the world and then walk away from it. Instead, You take an interest in my daily life and care about my eternal well-being.

I sometimes hesitate to offer praise because doing so implies that I understand enough of Your power to appreciate it. Despite this misgiving, may I always praise You for Your love, the grace of Jesus, and the guidance of the Holy Spirit.

FOR MERCY

Be merciful unto me, O Lord:
for I cry unto thee daily.
PSALM 86:3 KJV

Father, sometimes You seem to be far from me. I look and see a great abyss between us, but as I pray, my vision clears and I perceive a bridge that was there all along. It is a bridge of mercy, constructed by You. Thank You for building the bridge that connects me to the peace You provide.

Sometimes I think I am not worthy of mercy and question how You can offer it to me. Implant in me the understanding that to appreciate Your mercy, I must show mercy to others. Banish from my heart the evil thought that others are not worthy of Your forgiving compassion.

★ TOUCHING JESUS ★

*Finally, be ye all of one mind, having
compassion one of another, love as
brethren, be pitiful, be courteous.*
1 PETER 3:8 KJV

Lord Jesus, I read in the Bible that by coming to the
rescue of those who are hungry and thirsty, I am touch-
ing You. Help me never accept pain and suffering as a
natural condition. Guide me to show the compassion
that You had when You healed the sick and fed the
hungry multitudes. Help me put sympathy into action
for those who suffer.

Heavenly Father, I thank You for Your watchful eye
upon me. Guide me to bring a concrete expression
of love to others who have a physical or emotional
crisis. Provide me with the wisdom and the means to
relieve the suffering of others.

ASK, SEEK, KNOCK

*"Ask, and it will be given to you; seek, and you
will find; knock, and it will be opened to you.
For everyone who asks receives, and he who seeks
finds, and to him who knocks it will be opened."*

MATTHEW 7:7–8 NKJV

Generous God, it's hard for men to get it through their heads that Your Word teaches You *want* to bless guys who love You and come to You with their requests. I love You, Lord, but sometimes I wonder if I should really keep coming to You until I receive what I know You want to give me. I humbly ask that You give me the confidence I need to approach You, hands outstretched to receive what I need.

⟺ INDUSTRIAL-STRENGTH BLEACH ⟺

Come now, and let us reason together,
saith the LORD: though your sins be as scarlet,
they shall be as white as snow; though they
be red like crimson, they shall be as wool.

ISAIAH 1:18 KJV

Father, sometimes I place a pen in my shirt pocket without retracting the point. The mistake causes a prominent ink stain on my shirt. The garment is ruined, only to be worn when I am doing grubby chores.

Unlike the shirt, dear Lord, You are able and willing to cleanse my life that has been tarnished by worldly ambitions. Please remove every sin from my life so that my soul will be white as snow. Remove all bitterness and every desire to do evil. Thank You for creating in me a pure heart, O Lord.

TRUST IN GOD

God is our refuge and strength, a very present help in trouble. Therefore will not we fear, though the earth be removed, and though the mountains be carried into the midst of the sea.

Psalm 46:1–2 KJV

Father, I prayed for You to quell the doubts and fears that troubled my mind. You gave me guidance to overcome those events that were in my power to change. You gave me the emotional soundness to bear the trials that remained. I see now that You put them there so that, by enduring them, I would gain character and confidence.

Lord, help me recognize the distress of others when they are in a valley. Help me understand their pain and support them through their dark days. Give me the wisdom to be an encouragement to them. May I learn to put my trust in You and succeed in sharing that trust with others.

KILL 'EM WITH KINDNESS

*Therefore "If your enemy is hungry, feed him;
if he is thirsty, give him a drink; for in so doing
you will heap coals of fire on his head." Do not be
overcome by evil, but overcome evil with good.*
ROMANS 12:20–21 NKJV

Lord, I've heard it said that the best way to deal with someone who is angry at me, or someone who just doesn't like me, is to "kill them with kindness"—meaning I should speak kind words or do nice deeds in an effort to ease those negative feelings. I know that showing kindness toward an antagonist won't literally kill that person. But it just might foster peace, and maybe even a friendship, between us. Who knows? It might even open the door to a conversation about You.

WIN/WIN

*As every man hath received the gift, even so
minister the same one to another, as good
stewards of the manifold grace of God.*

1 PETER 4:10 KJV

★ ★ ★

Lord Most High, sometimes I allow my future to be
determined by others. I become dependent upon them
to guide me and to take the lead in solving my problems. At other times I try to be totally independent of
others and chart my own course. I fail to recognize that
You have made human beings to be interdependent.
I understand this concept as it applies to the church,
my marriage, and family.

Lord, may I recognize the advantages of shared
action in my daily contact with other people. I pray
that I will not think others must lose in order for me
to win. Instead, guide me to succeed in cooperative
endeavors that bring glory to Your kingdom.

OUTWARDLY FOCUSED

*Do nothing out of selfish ambition or vain
conceit. Rather, in humility value others above
yourselves, not looking to your own interests
but each of you to the interests of the others.*

PHILIPPIANS 2:3–4 NIV

Heavenly Father, I confess to You that I can be a selfish
man. Even when I do things that look like they're in
service to You, I'm often serving myself. Humble me
and change my heart so that everything I do comes
from a desire to serve You first, others second, and
myself last. Show me today specifically how I can be
more outwardly focused. Give me opportunities to
care for the interests and needs of others in my sphere
of influence. And help me do that with an unselfish
spirit, a heart clean of any selfish ambition.

RECHARGE

*Be of good courage, and he shall strengthen
your heart, all ye that hope in the LORD.*
PSALM 31:24 KJV

Lord, when my car doesn't start because the battery is dead, I get a jump start and recharge it. But why did it run down? Did I leave the lights on, was there a hidden drain on the battery, or did the battery itself have a bad cell?

Father, sometimes I am drained of strength. Thank You for providing opportunities for me to be recharged by plugging into prayer, Bible study, and fellowship with other Christians. Help me discover the reason that I have become spiritually exhausted. Renew me and help me keep Your abundant power.

CLOTHED IN HUMILITY

*All of you, clothe yourselves with humility
toward one another, because, "God opposes
the proud but shows favor to the humble."
Humble yourselves, therefore, under God's mighty
hand, that he may lift you up in due time.*

1 PETER 5:5–6 NIV

★ ★ ★

Mighty God, I confess that my human pride sometimes shows itself in how I interact with others. I know You call me to be a humble man, and I know You want that humility to demonstrate itself so that others can see it. Your servant Peter wrote that I should "clothe" myself in humility. That, Lord, tells me that every day I need to *choose* to wear humility—like a jacket. I need to willfully choose to treat others as more important than myself. Father, remind me to do just that every morning—and to make sure I never take off my jacket of humility during the day.

STAYING CONNECTED

*And he is the head of the body, the church:
who is the beginning, the firstborn from the dead;
that in all things he might have the preeminence.*
COLOSSIANS 1:18 KJV

I feel more connected to You, Jesus, when I fellowship with other believers. The house of God provides a plot of fertile soil where my knowledge of You can grow and my soul can be refreshed. Each time I attend church, I acknowledge You as my Savior. It is one way I demonstrate to others my commitment to You.

Lord, I pray I will always look to You as the head of the Church.

READY WITH AN ANSWER

*But sanctify the Lord God in your hearts,
and always be ready to give a defense to
everyone who asks you a reason for the hope
that is in you, with meekness and fear.*

1 PETER 3:15 NKJV

Lord Jesus, I confess that I don't always make the best of every opportunity to tell other men about You. It's not that I'm ashamed of You, and it's not just that I'm shy. Sometimes I wonder if I can answer the tough questions a non-believing friend may throw my way. I want to overcome my reluctance, and I know the only way to do that is to understand You and Your message even better than I do now. Prepare me, Lord, because I don't want to miss out on even one opportunity to help bring someone into Your kingdom.

HUSBAND

Nevertheless let every one of you in particular
so love his wife even as himself; and the wife
see that she reverence her husband.

EPHESIANS 5:33 KJV

Lord, I've heard that a husband prays for You to keep his wife the sweet person he married, and a wife prays for You to change her husband into the man she wants him to be. Instead, I pray that You will make us what You want us to be.

I am thankful, Lord, that I married the woman I loved, and today I can say I love the woman I married. I pray that I will respect her as a faithful partner and that we may walk side by side in the path You direct.

CASTING MY VOTE

*If my people, which are called by my name,
shall humble themselves, and pray, and seek
my face, and turn from their wicked ways;
then will I hear from heaven, and will
forgive their sin, and will heal their land.*

2 CHRONICLES 7:14 KJV

Dear Lord, at each election I cast my ballot and wear the sticker that says "I voted." When I think about my Christian service, I realize that my most influential vote is the way that I live. Each day I make choices: the products I buy, the television programs I surf through, and the church activities I participate in. I vote by my attitudes and actions.

I pray I will vote for justice, honesty, and moral responsibility, not only in the ballot box but also in the daily choices that I make.

KNOWING THE TRUTH
ABOUT YOURSELF

*Here is a trustworthy saying that deserves full
acceptance: Christ Jesus came into the world to
save sinners—of whom I am the worst. But for that
very reason I was shown mercy so that in me, the
worst of sinners, Christ Jesus might display his
immense patience as an example for those who
would believe in him and receive eternal life.*

1 TIMOTHY 1:15–16 NIV

God of grace, I often hear that I need to think highly of
myself, that a positive self-image is the key to a happy
and successful life. But I know better. So do You. Help
me always to remember that my true value is found
in the fact that You loved me so much that Jesus came
to earth and lived, died, and rose from the dead so
that my many sins can be forgiven.

WORSHIP

Nevertheless he left not himself without witness, in that he did good, and gave us rain from heaven, and fruitful seasons, filling our hearts with food and gladness.

ACTS 14:17 KJV

★ ★ ★

Heavenly Father, I looked out this morning to see a steady, soaking rain. I thought of my parched yard and how much the grass needed the precipitation. Within a few minutes, the blades of grass appeared green and glistened with healthy life. Lord, sometimes I become spiritually dry. Like a drought, the condition creeps in slowly, over time. Before my strength grows weak, please send heavenly water to refresh my soul and rejuvenate my worship. I pray that I will always be receptive to You and that Your abundant blessings will continue to shower down on me.

"ONE ANOTHER"

*And let us consider how we may spur one another
on toward love and good deeds, not giving up
meeting together, as some are in the habit of
doing, but encouraging one another—and all
the more as you see the Day approaching.*
HEBREWS 10:24–25 NIV

Lord, Your Word repeatedly confirms how important
it is that I spend time with other believers. You've
put me in a circle of fellowship so that my brothers
and I can love one another, encourage one another,
serve one another, and challenge one another. Yes,
there are times when it's just You and me, with no one
else around. Those times are vitally important to me
as I grow in my relationship with You. But I also need
to spend time with other believers. Help me to train
my mind toward giving and receiving blessings as I
spend time with fellow followers of Christ.

RESPECT

He that followeth after righteousness and mercy
findeth life, righteousness, and honour.
PROVERBS 21:21 KJV

★ ★ ★

Lord, although I do not often acknowledge it, I realize that my wife's respect is important to me. I see other men who are devastated when they lose the respect of someone they cherish. I have heard that, for some men, being respected is more important than being loved. "Not me, Lord," I say. But I know I can be shattered by a word rashly spoken, especially by my wife.

I pray that I will inspire respect by making sacrifices. Remove from me the idea that my sense of purpose depends on how others view me. Replace it with a concern for how You regard me.

BEING WITH BELIEVERS

I was glad when they said unto me,
Let us go into the house of the LORD.
Psalm 122:1 KJV

★　★　★

Heavenly Father, reading the Bible, talking to You in prayer, singing hymns, and meeting with other Christians help fortify my spiritual life. Only by becoming strong in You can I overcome obstacles. I need to assemble with other Christians because I gain strength by associating with those who love You. Our singing, praying, and study of Your Word inspire me to a closer walk with You.

Heavenly Father, I need the fellowship of dedicated believers. Help me realize that they need me too because we are blessed through fellowship with others.

★ A BLESSED INVITATION ★

Then the angel said to me, "Write this:
Blessed are those who are invited to the
wedding supper of the Lamb!" And he added,
"These are the true words of God."
REVELATION 19:9 NIV

Lord Jesus, I've been to many weddings, and I've noticed something: While a wedding is a solemn ceremony in which two people vow to spend the rest of their lives together, it's also a festive occasion. The reception that follows is a time when friends and family members join the bride and groom to eat, drink, dance, and offer their congratulations. Lord, You've offered me a special invitation to the greatest wedding feast of all time. Not only that, I'll be one of the guests of honor! Help me to live daily in the assurance that I'll one day attend the party to end all parties.

A READY HARVEST

*Pray ye therefore the Lord of the harvest, that
he will send forth labourers into his harvest.*
MATTHEW 9:38 KJV

Father, even from my limited gardening experience, I've seen that weeds grow without encouragement, but good crops require attention. Seeds must be planted in soil that has been prepared to receive them, weeds must be eliminated, and produce must be harvested at the right time.

Almighty Savior, I see that the same sequence is necessary to produce a spiritual harvest. Lord, make me a faithful worker in Your harvest. Help me to be diligent in the work that brings the lost to You. May I have an urgency to gather souls into Your kingdom before the season is past and the crop is lost.

Day 302

A BOOK I CAN TRUST

No prophecy of Scripture is of any private interpretation, for prophecy never came by the will of man, but holy men of God spoke as they were moved by the Holy Spirit.

2 PETER 1:20–21 NKJV

Thank You, God, for going to such amazing lengths to give me the Bible. I know I can trust Your written Word because Your own Holy Spirit inspired men of Your own choosing to write it. The words of this book reflect Your heart. They give me Your every promise, every command, and every bit of wisdom I need to live a life of faith that pleases You. I confess that sometimes I don't read Your Word as regularly as I should. Help me make time in Your Word a daily priority.

KEEPING A COOL HEAD

Don't be quick to fly off the handle.
Anger boomerangs. You can spot a
fool by the lumps on his head.
ECCLESIASTES 7:9 MSG

God of peace, I try not to be a hot-headed man. But I confess that there are times when I lose my temper and do and say things that don't please You. Forgive me for my anger and help me to keep a cool head when some provokes me, even unintentionally. Help me to respond to provocations in a loving way, but if I do become angry, help me to reconcile with the other person quickly. I know anger itself isn't a sin, but losing my temper is. And I don't want to dishonor You by displaying unrighteous anger.

ASKING FOR DIRECTIONS

*For even hereunto were ye called: because
Christ also suffered for us, leaving us an
example, that ye should follow his steps.*
1 PETER 2:21 KJV

★ ★ ★

Lord, I would rather drive in circles for an hour than stop for five minutes to ask for directions. Usually I end up with only some lost time, but on some occasions I've ended up in areas that I would normally avoid.

Sometimes I wander around spiritually too. Because I refuse to ask for directions, I find myself in places that I should avoid. Father, I pray that I may be willing to ask for Your guidance and follow it. Protect me from self-reliance and arrogance. Direct me to Your truth and help me act according to Your guidance.

COMPLEX TO SIMPLE

*I will greatly rejoice in the LORD, my soul shall
be joyful in my God; for he hath clothed me
with the garments of salvation, he hath covered
me with the robe of righteousness, as a
bridegroom decketh himself with ornaments.*

ISAIAH 61:10 KJV

Father, I see the wonder of Your creation in all of its
complexity, and I bow before You in humble adoration.
When I study the world You have created, I cannot
but admire how the complex parts work together as
a simple whole.

When I read the Bible and study Your Word, it
is at first a complex story that spans the ages. But
then I see Your guiding hand behind the events that
brought Jesus into this world, and I see how His death
and resurrection give salvation to those who simply
accept You by faith. I admire and honor You for giving
me a simple salvation plan, one that I can comprehend.

Day 306

QUALIFIED TO DO YOUR PART

There are different kinds of gifts, but the same Spirit distributes them. There are different kinds of service, but the same Lord. There are different kinds of working, but in all of them and in everyone it is the same God at work.

1 CORINTHIANS 12:4–6 NIV

Father in heaven, You've called many people who didn't necessarily believe they were qualified to serve. I remember Moses, who didn't think his status or oratorical skills were good enough. Lord, I want to serve You and others, but I know I can only do that when You empower and equip me. Show me what You want me to do for You, and then, when I question whether I am qualified to serve, remind me that Your Holy Spirit gives me everything I need. You will empower me to make a difference in my congregation and in the world around me.

NOTHING NEW

I have seen all the works that are done under the sun; and, behold, all is vanity and vexation of spirit.
ECCLESIASTES 1:14 KJV

Each day, Lord, I am bombarded with advertisements. Embedded in the glittering generalities is the assurance that the merchandise is on the leading edge. The fashion models are chosen because of their appeal to the young and vigorous. I suddenly discover a product that is essential, although I have been getting along without it all of my life. I disparage as outdated my perfectly serviceable possessions.

Heavenly Father, I pray that I will not allow advertisements to exploit my tendency to be discontented. Help me dismiss sales pitches that appeal to desire and pride. Keep me away from the idea that I can improve my future with things rather than by living for You.

LIVING IN CHRIST

So then, just as you received Christ Jesus as Lord, continue to live your lives in him, rooted and built up in him, strengthened in the faith as you were taught, and overflowing with thankfulness.
COLOSSIANS 2:6–7 NIV

★ ★ ★

Lord Jesus Christ, thank You for coming to earth to live, die, and be raised from the dead so that I could be brought into Your eternal kingdom. But I confess that I am often torn: On one hand, I want to do what pleases me, but on the other, I want to live in a way that glorifies and pleases You. Help me to grow in my faith in You, my love for You, and my gratitude over all You've done for me. When these things fill my heart, my overcoming desire is to live for You and in You. Fill my heart, Lord.

RIGHTEOUSNESS

*And the L<small>ORD</small> said unto Noah, Come thou
and all thy house into the ark; for thee have I
seen righteous before me in this generation.*
G<small>ENESIS</small> 7:1 KJV

Lord, sometimes I look around and see all kinds of sin
in this world. I let my guard down, and I am tempted
to say or do something I know is wrong. In moments
like that, I remember the account of Noah. He refused
to compromise his righteous walk with You, Lord. The
evil people of his day mocked him as he built the ark,
but You honored his righteousness by saving him and
his family from the flood.

Dear God, help me to find favor in Your eyes by
maintaining Christian traits. The most important concern in my life is to please You.

THE AMAZING POWER
AND LOVE OF GOD

*"Ah, Sovereign LORD, you have made the
heavens and the earth by your great power and
outstretched arm. Nothing is too hard for you."*
JEREMIAH 32:17 NIV

Lord God, as a mere man I am severely limited in what
I have the power to do. I can't change people's hearts, I
can't arrange events in this world, I can't make the dead
live, and I can't rescue anyone from the consequences
of sin. But You can. You are my Creator—the Creator
of the whole universe—and there is nothing You can't
do. I can't fully comprehend Your incredible power. I
stand amazed that a God of such might actually cares
for such an insignificant creature as me. Thank You for
being big enough and powerful enough to create all
I see, yet kind and loving enough to reach down to
me individually.

FATHER

The father of the righteous shall greatly rejoice: and he that begetteth a wise child shall have joy of him.
PROVERBS 23:24 KJV

Heavenly Father, I am perplexed by how the world sees fathers. In the old television shows, the man of the house was a wise, successful, and morally superior father. Today, the father is often portrayed as a bewildered but lovable buffoon who hasn't the foggiest notion of how to solve the problems his children face.

Father, I pray I can be like You in the essential points. Lead me to carry out the central duties of a father: providing care, love, protection, and guidance. Even when my children are not present, I desire my actions to be those of a godly father. Most important of all, I want to be the cornerstone of a righteous family.

Day 312

ON THE FRONT LINE

And how shall they preach, except they be sent? as it is written, How beautiful are the feet of them that preach the gospel of peace, and bring glad tidings of good things!
ROMANS 10:15 KJV

Good Shepherd, I pray for the missionaries who teach the Gospel at the risk of their own lives. I cannot help but admire and support those brave individuals who are willing to follow that calling. May they radiate the Gospel by both their words and deeds to the destitute, sick, suffering, and spiritually barren.

Lord, may their example encourage me to support those who step out in faith so they will be fully equipped to effectively spread the Gospel to the world. Help them be full of energy. Protect them from those who resent their efforts.

GIVING AND RECEIVING

*Give generously to them and do so without
a grudging heart; then because of this the
LORD your God will bless you in all your work
and in everything you put your hand to.*

DEUTERONOMY 15:10 NIV

Giving God, I confess that I'm not always the most generous giver. My lack of generosity is often based on fear—I want to hang on to what I have so I won't come up short when it's time to pay bills and buy the things my family needs. I know this demonstrates a lack of faith in You and in Your willingness and ability to keep Your promises. Forgive me, Lord! You tell me that when I give out of a pure heart of generosity, You will take care of me and bless me. Remind me often that You keep *all* Your promises.

BEYOND PETITION

Praying always with all prayer and supplication in the Spirit, and watching thereunto with all perseverance and supplication for all saints.
EPHESIANS 6:18 KJV

Father, although I pray with a submissive spirit, this matter is such a burden on my heart that it rises above a petition. I often pray from the intellect, without feeling emotion. My supplication this time is from a heart so burdened that I cannot find the words to express my needs.

I come before You in all humility and exhaustion. I am earnestly seeking Your mercy and compassion. Although things look bleak, I know You will show me a way through. Help me emerge on the other side with a stronger faith.

DELIVERED FROM DISCOURAGEMENT

The righteous cry out, and the LORD hears them;
he delivers them from all their troubles.
The LORD is close to the brokenhearted and
saves those who are crushed in spirit.
PSALM 34:17–18 NIV

Father in heaven, I believe it when You tell me that You are with me, even when I have reason to feel down and discouraged. Lord, life here on earth is hard—and in some ways it's even harder for a man of God who is focused on hearing and obeying Your instructions for a life that pleases You. I want to be that kind of man, but there are so many pressures around me— so many barriers in my way. Thank You, God, for Your promise to be there for me, to hear me when I bring my discouragement and troubles to You.

MINISTERS

*And my speech and my preaching was not
with enticing words of man's wisdom, but in
demonstration of the Spirit and of power.*
1 CORINTHIANS 2:4 KJV

I come before You, Lord, asking that Your protection
would be upon the ministers of the Gospel in this
community. I ask You to raise up people with vision
who can solve the difficulties of today and anticipate
the problems of tomorrow. Help them have the wisdom to speak for You in love. Build a protective fence
around them so they are left unscathed by those who
belittle their efforts.

Father, I pray that I will do all I can to support those
who bring Your Word to my community. May I stand
with them so they have the courage to deliver Your
message untainted by secular concerns.

DIVINE FORGETFULNESS

"No longer will they teach their neighbor, or say to one another, 'Know the LORD,' because they will all know me, from the least of them to the greatest," declares the LORD. "For I will forgive their wickedness and will remember their sins no more."

JEREMIAH 31:34 NIV

God of forgiveness, it's so hard for me to think of You as forgetful. Yet You've promised that once I've confessed my sins and received Your forgiveness, You no longer give thought to my past. In fact, Jeremiah 31:34 assures me that You don't even remember them. Lord, help me to forget my mistakes and put my past behind me. I know You have. And who am I to hang on to things You've already chosen to forget?

AGGRESSIVE FAITH

*I can do all things through
Christ which strengtheneth me.*
PHILIPPIANS 4:13 KJV

Father, I go out each day as a soldier for You. If I am rewarded with victory after victory, may I examine my goals in case I am aiming too low. Teach me to see clearly the battles You want me to fight. Give me the ability to think the impossible, and fill me with the aggressive faith to make it happen.

Battles are long and victories are short. I would rather enjoy victories than failure, but I would rather suffer a lost battle than stand on the sidelines and do nothing. Almighty God, I surrender myself to Your service.

TRUSTING ENOUGH TO GIVE

"Bring the whole tithe into the storehouse, that there may be food in my house. Test me in this," says the LORD Almighty, "and see if I will not throw open the floodgates of heaven and pour out so much blessing that there will not be room enough to store it."

MALACHI 3:10 NIV

Lord, You command me in Your Word to give generously, and You have promised me great blessings when I obey. Yet I often find it difficult to open my wallet and give toward Your continued work here on earth. I believe my reluctance to give has less to do with simple selfishness and more to do with a lack of trust in You to provide what I need to care for my family. Father, forgive me for my lack of generosity. Forgive me for not trusting You enough to give out of what You've given me.

Day 320

HYPOCRISY

Let no man despise thy youth; but be thou an
example of the believers, in word, in conversation,
in charity, in spirit, in faith, in purity.
1 TIMOTHY 4:12 KJV

★ ★ ★

Heavenly Father, I pray I never become a deceiver who tries to live two lives. Good cannot exist at the same time as deception. For if I live two lives, one of them must die. I pray that it is the false life, the hypocritical one, that dies.

Lord, although I cannot achieve the sinless life of Christ, help me follow Your Word so closely that I illustrate a true Christian life. I pray that my example is not a poor copy but an original born in Your likeness, educated in Your love, and reflecting Your grandeur.

THE OBJECT OF YOUR TRUST

*Trust in the L*ORD *with all your heart and lean not on your own understanding; in all your ways submit to him, and he will make your paths straight.*
PROVERBS 3:5–6 NIV

God, it's not always easy for me to trust another person completely, because even the best people I know have moments when they prove themselves less than perfectly worthy. But it's not that way with You. Thank You, Lord, that I can always count on You. You have proven Yourself trustworthy, not just in the lives of all the saints before me, but in my own life as well. Help me always to remember Your trustworthiness, especially when I need encouragement, comfort, or direction. Help me to look beyond my own circumstances and trust You fully to guide and direct me.

THE THIRD ROAD

*Open to me the gates of righteousness: I will go
into them, and I will praise the LORD: this gate
of the LORD, into which the righteous shall enter.*
PSALM 118:19–20 KJV

Heavenly Father, I read in Your Word about two roads—
one to destruction and one to eternal life. In my ignorance, I seek a third road built especially for me. It's a
comfortable way—one that accommodates an agreeable husband, dutiful father, dependable employee,
and occasional community volunteer. It requires only
halfhearted service to You without the full acceptance
of the blood of Jesus.

Lord, I do realize that there are two roads, not
three. The road I take depends on the gate that I
walk through. Lord, guide me through the gate that
leads to eternal life.

GUIDANCE

*For thou art my rock and my fortress; therefore
for thy name's sake lead me, and guide me.*
PSALM 31:3 KJV

Lord, I sometimes look at every event as either a positive or negative, an advance toward a goal or a detour away from it. I wonder why a promotion did not occur or why, if it did, it had unforeseen negative consequences.

Dear Lord, let me never become so determined to reach my goal that I fail to see Your hand guiding my life in the plan that You have set for me. May I continue to set short-term goals and make long-range plans but temper my expectations with thought and prayer.

TRUE CONFESSION

"The Pharisee stood by himself and prayed: 'God, I thank you that I am not like other people—robbers, evildoers, adulterers—or even like this tax collector.' . . . But the tax collector stood at a distance. He would not even look up to heaven, but beat his breast and said, 'God, have mercy on me, a sinner.'"

LUKE 18:11–13 NIV

My Savior Jesus, it's ironic that You call me to be more like a man who was considered the worst of sinners during Your time on earth and less like a man people believed was among God's most devout servants. But the tax collector in Your story is just the kind of man You call me to be—a man who knows he needs Your mercy and forgiveness. Keep me humble, Lord, by reminding me often that I'm saved not because I avoid certain sins but because of Your amazing love.

GIVING OF MYSELF

And whosoever will be chief among you,
let him be your servant: even as the Son of
man came not to be ministered unto, but to
minister, and to give his life a ransom for many.
MATTHEW 20:27–28 KJV

As I contemplate all the activities that demand my attention, I think of You, Jesus. You did the work of a servant by washing the feet of the apostles. Please help me remember that the greatest in the kingdom of heaven is not the one being served, but the humble one doing the serving.

Sometimes I find it easier to give from a distance than to become personally involved in situations. Help me, Lord, to fulfill the mission to serve others. I need Your strength to meet my obligations to my family, my coworkers, and members of my community.

STANDING IN THE GAP

*"I looked for someone among them who
would build up the wall and stand before me
in the gap on behalf of the land so I would
not have to destroy it, but I found no one."*
 EZEKIEL 22:30 NIV

★ ★ ★

Holy Father, when I look around me and see the state
of the world today, there are so many people who seem
hopeless—due to their own choices or due to what has
been done to them. But You are a God who delights in
changing hearts and transforming lives. You are a God
who saves the irredeemable and heals the hopelessly
sick. Thank You for the privilege of begging Your mercy,
forgiveness, and healing for those who can't or don't
pray for themselves. Let me be a man who consistently
stands in the gap on behalf of others.

MATERIAL WEALTH

Let your conversation be without covetousness; and be content with such things as ye have: for he hath said, I will never leave thee, nor forsake thee.

HEBREWS 13:5 KJV

Dear Lord, You know I worry about money. Not because I am afraid I will not have enough, but because of my concern for those who depend upon me. I feel a strong obligation to provide for my family.

Lord, prevent me from using my role as a provider to rationalize an excessive devotion to making money. I pray that I will never measure success by material wealth or possessions, or think of money as a symbol of my worth. Thank You for assuring me that You will provide for my needs.

FAITH DEFINED

*Now faith is confidence in what we hope
for and assurance about what we do not see.
This is what the ancients were commended for.*

HEBREWS 11:1–2 NIV

★ ★ ★

Lord, I know that I can't please You without faith. I know that I must believe that You are and that You will reward me when I seek after You with everything I have. But sometimes I still have doubts. Sometimes I don't feel fully assured that You keep Your promises. Sometimes I feel like I need to see results before I fully believe. Father, help me not to become discouraged today but to continue trusting You and following You with everything I have. I will do that, trusting You to strengthen my faith and give me the assurance that You'll do what is best for me, even though I don't yet see it. Thank You for the gift of faith.

THE OBJECT OF YOUR LOVE

Do not love the world or anything in the world. If anyone loves the world, love for the Father is not in them. For everything in the world—the lust of the flesh, the lust of the eyes, and the pride of life—comes not from the Father but from the world.

1 JOHN 2:15–16 NIV

Lord Jesus, You once told Your followers that no one can serve two masters—because one will always pull our love and attention away from the other. In 1 John 2, Your Word tells me that I can't love You and the world at the same time. I have to live in this world, Lord, but I know that I can't love its ways. May my love be focused on You alone, so that my heart is never divided. I don't want to be tempted to serve anyone or anything but You.

FILLING UP WITH POWER

Strengthened with all might, according to his glorious power, unto all patience and longsuffering with joyfulness.
COLOSSIANS 1:11 KJV

Father, I watch with admiration as speedway pit crews service racecars. Drivers try to come in under a caution flag, but if there is no caution, they come in anyway for fuel, a change of tires, and minor repairs. They understand that even in the most tightly contested race, they must have regular pit stops.

Dear Lord, teach me to take the necessary breaks that give You time to make repairs in my heart and mind. When I fail to read the Bible and talk to You, my spiritual life runs low on power. In the race to heaven, keep me tuned up and filled with the faith I need to successfully finish my course.

LIGHT AND STRENGTH

The LORD is my light and my salvation;
whom shall I fear? The LORD is the strength
of my life; of whom shall I be afraid?
PSALM 27:1 NKJV

Father God, I live in a world of darkness, a world that doesn't know You or honor You—and the results speak for themselves. At times I feel overwhelmed at this darkness, and it seems that nothing within me can overcome it. Lord, I need Your light to guide my way, and I need Your strength to help me withstand everything that the father of lies throws at me. In many ways, Satan holds dominion over this dark world. But You, Lord, have dominion over him—You are in control of all things. With You as my light and strength, I have nothing to fear in this life.

PERSEVERING IN PRAYER

He touched the socket of his hip; and the socket of Jacob's hip was out of joint as He wrestled with him. And He said, "Let Me go, for the day breaks." But he said, "I will not let You go unless You bless me!"

Genesis 32:25–26 nkjv

God of all blessings, I am humbled and challenged when I read of Your servant clinging to You and refusing to let go until You blessed him. May I show that kind of persistence and perseverance as I seek blessings from You. Father, I know You want to bless me in all I do for You, for that is one of the ways You are glorified in me. May I never give up or become discouraged as I come to You and ask for what I know You want to give me.

EYES FORWARD

I will lift up mine eyes unto the hills, from whence cometh my help. My help cometh from the LORD, which made heaven and earth.

PSALM 121:1–2 KJV

Father, I become distracted by events that take place around me. But when I turn my eyes toward You, I can see that enduring the trials of this life are well worth where You are taking me.

Sometimes my prayers are filled with concerns. I come with intercession for others, a petition for my own needs, and an entreaty for forgiveness. Build in me the assurance that You are sympathetic toward the matters that I bring before You. I know that comfort is only a prayer away. Thank You for listening to my appeal.

WAITING FOR
STRENGTH AND POWER

*He gives power to the weak, and to those who
have no might He increases strength. Even the
youths shall faint and be weary, and the young
men shall utterly fall, but those who wait on the
LORD shall renew their strength; they shall mount
up with wings like eagles, they shall run and not
be weary, they shall walk and not faint.*

ISAIAH 40:29–31 NKJV

God of power and might, I confess that I'm not always
as patient as You call me to be. Sometimes, when I see
a task that needs doing—even one You've specifically
called me to accomplish—I can run out ahead and
attack it rather than wait on You. But I've learned that
when I do that, my strength quickly dries up and I
burn out. Lord, give me the wisdom to wait for You to
give me the go-ahead and the empowerment I need
to accomplish something great for You.

A LIVING STONE

Ye also, as lively stones, are built up a spiritual house, an holy priesthood, to offer up spiritual sacrifices, acceptable to God by Jesus Christ.

1 PETER 2:5 KJV

Lord, I am amazed at the ceaseless action of waves. I find stones that are rounded smooth by the continuous pounding of the water. Even the edges of broken glass are smoothed away until they are no longer sharp.

Father, I see Your ceaseless action on my life in the same way. Day by day, You remove my rough edges. You blunt my sharp tongue, soften my overbearing manner, cool my hot temper, and smooth out my uneven disposition. From a rough and unremarkable stone, You have made me into something better. Thank You for continuously changing me.

FOR UNITY OF BELIEVERS

And the glory which thou gavest me I have given them; that they may be one, even as we are one.
JOHN 17:22 KJV

Righteous Father, I am humbled when I realize that Jesus, on the night He was betrayed, prayed for the unity of believers. I look at Your Word through different eyes than other Christians and often cannot fully agree with them. Help me focus on our many vital common beliefs rather than our few trivial differences. Help me see the strength in unity and the danger of discord.

Often it is easy to agree if the agreement is to do nothing. Let my agreement be to act and do, not sit back and wait. Let me join the fellowship of believers so we become a force for righteousness.

CLOTHED IN LOVE

Therefore, as God's chosen people, holy and dearly loved, clothe yourselves with compassion, kindness, humility, gentleness and patience.
COLOSSIANS 3:12 NIV

God of love, I confess that I don't always do a good job of demonstrating Your love to those around me—especially to those outside the faith. I sometimes think judgmental thoughts, and I don't always show kindness to those who don't know You. Instead, I can be proud, harsh, and impatient. Forgive me, Lord, and help me to be a better example of Your love. When men look down on me, let it be because I serve You with my whole heart, and not because I'm harsh and judgmental. Let others see a living, growing example of the kind of love You poured out on me, even before I knew You.

GOOD AND PERFECT GIFTS

*Every good and perfect gift is from above, coming
down from the Father of the heavenly lights,
who does not change like shifting shadows.*

JAMES 1:17 NIV

Perfect Father, You tell me in Your Word that You hate
human pride—that You actively oppose those with
arrogant hearts and minds. Lord, remind me often
that every good thing I have and every good thing I
accomplish in this life are the result of Your generosity
toward me. The enemy of my soul wants me to believe
that I should feel pride over my accomplishments. He
wants me to feel pride in what I do, what I earn, and
what I have. But all those things are gifts from You, my
generous Father in heaven. Thank You for all these
things and more.

CORROSION RESISTANT

*Woe unto you, scribes and Pharisees, hypocrites!
for ye are like unto whited sepulchres, which indeed
appear beautiful outward, but are within full of
dead men's bones, and of all uncleanness.*

MATTHEW 23:27 KJV

★ ★ ★

Dear Lord, I can tell when iron becomes rusty because the color of the rust is different from the color of the metal. I understand, however, that some metals have rust that is the same color as the underlying metal. The metal continues to weaken, yet there is no outward sign of the problem.

Jesus, I pray that You will come to my rescue when sin attacks me. Open my eyes so that I will see my transgressions and avoid them in the future. Lord, guard me from the sin that can reach below the surface. Keep my life free from corruption.

═══ NO MERCY LIKE GOD'S MERCY ═══

Who is a God like You, pardoning iniquity and passing over the transgression of the remnant of His heritage? He does not retain His anger forever, because He delights in mercy.

MICAH 7:18 NKJV

Gracious, merciful Father, thank You for loving me and for joyfully showing me mercy when I sin against You. I have known men who hang on to their anger long after someone has done them wrong, even when the other person apologizes. But You, Lord, are not like that. You don't retain Your anger, though You would be just in doing so. You not only let go of Your anger and grant mercy to those in need, You actually take joy in doing so. Thank You for delighting in showing me mercy.

THE GOOD NEWS

How then will they call on Him in whom they have not believed? How will they believe in Him whom they have not heard? And how will they hear without a preacher? How will they preach unless they are sent? Just as it is written, "How beautiful are the feet of those who bring good news of good things!"

ROMANS 10:14–15 NASB

Savior and Lord, I'm amazed at how many people don't really understand who You are. They may know that You taught some great truths about life. They may even know that You claimed to be the Savior. But they don't have a clue about what those things should mean *to them*. Lord, give me a deep burden for those who need to hear about You, starting with the people in my own sphere of influence. Give me opportunities to share the best news of all time.

POISONOUS PRIDE

Human pride will be brought down, and human arrogance will be humbled. Only the LORD will be exalted on that day of judgment.

ISAIAH 2:11 NLT

Lord God, I confess that I'm sometimes tempted to become prideful. I want to rule my own life instead of letting You take charge. I want to depend on my own skills and abilities instead of turning them over to You and letting You use them to bless me. And I want to decide what is right and wrong for myself instead of relying on what You've told me in Your written Word. But that Word repeatedly tells me that You oppose human pride and bless humility. Lord, humble my heart before You. Help me to rely on You and live for You in every way.

AT MEALTIME

And God said, Behold, I have given you every herb bearing seed, which is upon the face of all the earth, and every tree, in the which is the fruit of a tree yielding seed; to you it shall be for meat.

GENESIS 1:29 KJV

I praise You, living God, who made all things. You spoke into existence the plant and animal kingdoms. You created a people in Your image to take care of Your creation.

Thank You, Lord, for the fruitful seasons that are made possible by Your design—the seasons of seedtime and harvest. I see eternity in the seeds of each fruit and vegetable because they ensure a harvest year after year. For the blessings of the dinner table, whether a simple staple like bread or a hearty main course, I give You praise, O Lord.

Day 344

═ THE GREATEST COMMANDMENT ═

Jesus said to him, "'You shall love the LORD your God with all your heart, with all your soul, and with all your mind.' This is the first and great commandment."

MATTHEW 22:37–38 NKJV

Lord God, after all You've done for me, loving You should come easily to me. But it doesn't always. Sometimes I neglect You, and other times I feel distant. Thank You, Jesus, for speaking this first and great commandment, for it reminds me that a life in You starts with my commitment to love the One who is so committed to me. Father, help me to love You more and more deeply every day, starting with today. Show me ways to express my love to You.

OVERCOMING DIFFICULTIES

"I've told you all this so that trusting me,
you will be unshakable and assured, deeply
at peace. In this godless world you will
continue to experience difficulties. But take
heart! I've conquered the world."

JOHN 16:33 MSG

Precious Jesus, I appreciate Your warning that I will have to endure difficulties. I've learned that trials are just part of living in a fallen world. But I thank You that You have promised me ultimate victory. I know that nothing will happen to me without Your approval, and I know that any suffering or trials I experience here on earth are part of Your ultimate plan. Lord, my difficulties look trivial when I compare them with what Your apostles endured. But I'm grateful that You care about them and that You've promised me ultimate victory.

★ CREATED TO WORK ★

The LORD God took the man and put him in the Garden of Eden to work it and take care of it.
GENESIS 2:15 NIV

Creator God, Genesis 2:15 tells me that You created me for a purpose: to work at accomplishing Your goals here on earth. Just as You put Adam in the Garden of Eden so he could work toward its upkeep, You've placed me where I work now to glorify You every day. Knowing that You created me to work gives the job I do, even the "secular" work, meaning and purpose. Empower me to glorify You as I labor, even when the tasks I'm assigned seem mundane. Thank You for giving me the ability to work and for allowing me to honor You as I do.

WALKING AS JESUS WALKED

Whoever keeps His word, in him the love of God has truly been perfected. By this we know that we are in Him: the one who says he abides in Him ought himself to walk in the same manner as He walked.

1 JOHN 2:5–6 NASB

Jesus, thank You for coming to earth and giving us the perfect example of how to live every day. I've personally known men who lived godly lives, but nobody did it better than You. You lived selflessly, but You also knew You needed time alone with Your Father. You reached out to sinners in the most personal way, but You never compromised on what was right. And You sacrificed everything, including Your very life, so that I could be drawn into Your heavenly family. Help me to walk like You, Jesus!

⸻ AN ALWAYS-PRESENT GOD ⸻

*Where can I go from your Spirit? Where
can I flee from your presence? If I go up
to the heavens, you are there; if I make
my bed in the depths, you are there.*

PSALM 139:7-8 NIV

Lord, I'm grateful that there is nowhere I can go and
nothing I can do to escape Your presence. You'll never
leave me on my own because You love me on such a
deep, personal level. Even in those times when I feel
like I'd like to be by myself a while, You are there.
During those times when I don't feel Your presence,
You are there. When my life circumstances cause me
to wonder if You have abandoned me, You are there.
Even when I am tempted to sin—even when I give in to
that temptation—You are there, drawing me back to You.

STRENGTH AND COURAGE

"Have I not commanded you? Be strong and courageous! Do not tremble or be dismayed, for the LORD your God is with you wherever you go."
JOSHUA 1:9 NASB

All-powerful God, I confess that I sometimes feel afraid. There have even been times when my fear all but paralyzed me. In Joshua 1:9, You told Your servant Joshua to be strong and courageous. But then You took that encouragement another huge step forward by telling Joshua he could be brave in the face of all potential dangers because You would always be with him. Lord, I believe that message is for me today too. When I feel afraid or anxious, remind me that You are and always will be with me. Help me to remember that You are bigger and mightier than any problem I'll ever face.

A GOD OF MERCY

"O my God, incline Your ear and hear; open Your eyes and see our desolations, and the city which is called by Your name; for we do not present our supplications before You because of our righteous deeds, but because of Your great mercies."

DANIEL 9:18 NKJV

★ ★ ★

Merciful, gracious God, thank You that the favor You so generously pour out on me has nothing to do with my performance or worthiness and everything to do with who You are. I sometimes fall into thinking that it's the other way around—that You only answer my prayers and bless me when I show myself worthy. Remind me often that You extend Your goodness to me only because You are so merciful and compassionate. That way, You, not I, receive the glory. Thank You for who You are.

══ A PERFECT EXAMPLE ══

"Whoever wants to become great among you must be your servant, and whoever wants to be first must be slave of all. For even the Son of Man did not come to be served, but to serve, and to give his life as a ransom for many."

MARK 10:43–45 NIV

Lord Jesus, You are the perfect example of a godly servant. You came to earth to do great things—to teach, to preach, and to rebuke those You knew were wrong. But more than that, You came to serve—and serve to the point of giving up Your very life so that others could live forever. I know, Jesus, that You want me to do great works for You. Let those things flow from my willingness to serve others first, just like You did.

★ SECURE IN JESUS ★

"And I give them eternal life, and they shall never perish; neither shall anyone snatch them out of My hand. My Father, who has given them to Me, is greater than all; and no one is able to snatch them out of My Father's hand."

JOHN 10:28–29 NKJV

Lord Jesus, I thank You for holding me securely in Your hand. Sometimes, I don't feel as secure as John 10 tells me I should. But I know that when I don't feel secure in You, it's most likely because *I've* drifted—I'm not abiding in You as I should. Draw me nearer to You, for that is where I feel secure, loved, and part of Your eternal family. Thank You for saving me and making me one of Your own.

THE POWER OF THE WORD

For our gospel came not unto you in word only,
but also in power, and in the Holy Ghost, and in
much assurance; as ye know what manner of
men we were among you for your sake.

1 THESSALONIANS 1:5 KJV

Lord, I confess to You that I often read the Bible hurriedly and without much comprehension. Despite my sometimes superficial reading, I do gain something from staying in touch with You. More gratifying, though, are those occasions when I take the time to think upon Your Word and meditate upon Your message. Most useful of all are those occasions when certain passages capture my attention. For several days I carry the verses around in my thoughts and pray about them. Slowly, by continually holding them in my mind, they dawn into full light. Father, I pray that the power of Your Word will transform my mind. Change the printed words into words written on my heart and living in my spirit.

★ A CLUTTERED MIND ★

*Wherefore seeing we also are compassed
about with so great a cloud of witnesses,
let us lay aside every weight, and the sin
which doth so easily beset us, and let us run
with patience the race that is set before us.*

HEBREWS 12:1 KJV

Father, I'm trying to clean out the garage again. It is amazing the amount of clutter that accumulates in a year's time. Sometimes I become emotionally involved with inanimate objects and delay letting them go. Yet, I discard them when I realize they are taking up space without providing any benefit. In the same way, I pray I will frequently take a spiritual inventory and make a determined effort to eliminate the mental clutter from my life. Many items need to be set aside: prejudices, dependencies, destructive relationships, jealousies, irrational fears, and memories of past failures. Father, rather than merely moving this clutter to a temporary storage place, help me abandon it entirely.

IN THE MORNING

This is the day which the LORD hath made;
we will rejoice and be glad in it.
PSALM 118:24 KJV

Good morning, Lord. As my first talk with You today, I want to thank You for giving me another day. I don't know what it holds, but I am thankful that I have another opportunity to live for You.

Later I'll bring to You those specific needs that arise each day. I will speak the names of people who need Your special touch. Now, however, I give You thanks and I praise You. More than anything else, I want to acknowledge who You are and not just what You have done. You are the reason I get up each morning.

Day 356

IN THE EVENING

*Let my prayer be set forth before thee
as incense; and the lifting up of my
hands as the evening sacrifice.*
PSALM 141:2 KJV

Lord, I have seen relationships dissolve because of a failure to communicate. The lack of an interchange of thoughts and information caused erosion in the friendly camaraderie.

I ask that You will help me to relate well with my family and associates. On a spiritual level, I pray that my heavenly communication keeps a clear line of sending and receiving messages from You. In this evening prayer, I want to evaluate my relationship with You. Staying in contact with You, Lord, has the eternal importance of helping me realize my blessings and translating them into actions to share with others.

DESTROYING DARKNESS

*For the commandment is a lamp;
and the law is light; and reproofs
of instruction are the way of life.*
PROVERBS 6:23 KJV

Dear Father, every time I replace a lightbulb, I wonder why it burned out so quickly. Regardless of its limits, I am thankful for light that expels darkness.

Lord, because You used the example of light throughout scripture, I am able to understand Your holy character and comprehend the power that You have to destroy the darkness of sin. Jesus, let Your light shine through me so others will be exposed to the heavenly light that You delivered to earth long ago. I pray for Your guidance in my effort to share Your light with the lost world.

THE GOLDEN RULE

*Therefore all things whatsoever ye would that
men should do to you, do ye even so to them:
for this is the law and the prophets.*
MATTHEW 7:12 KJV

★ ★ ★

Lord, I have memorized the Bible verse that is called
the Golden Rule. Yet, putting it into practice is far more
difficult than learning the words. While You were here
on earth, You demonstrated the perfect example of
living out this principle.

Jesus, I praise You for showing me compassion
and granting me forgiveness for my transgressions.
Thank You for teaching me how to have peace in my
life. Lord, give me the determination to do unto others
as I want them to do unto me.

★ SACRIFICE OF PRAISE ★

*By him therefore let us offer the sacrifice
of praise to God continually, that is, the fruit
of our lips giving thanks to his name.*
HEBREWS 13:15 KJV

Lord, my life has been relatively devoid of the kinds
of sacrifices made by Christian pioneers of the past.
What sacrifices can I make?

Heavenly Father, I sacrifice to You my self-will.
To the one and only living God, I submit my life as an
offering of worship. Another sacrifice I offer is one
of praise. Purify my mouth that my praise may be
acceptable to You. I give thanks for Your redemption.
All praise, honor, and glory belong to You.

SACRIFICING FREEDOM

"I have the right to do anything," you say—but not everything is beneficial. "I have the right to do anything"—but not everything is constructive. No one should seek their own good, but the good of others.

1 CORINTHIANS 10:23–24 NIV

Loving heavenly Father, thank You for setting me free and allowing me to live in freedom. But even though I'm free from the bondage of living under a bunch of rules, I know I am to live my life in a way that glorifies You and benefits other men—believers and non-believers alike. Lord, give me a heart that is willing to sacrifice its own desires—even those that aren't necessarily sinful—for the good of my brothers in Christ and of those who don't yet know You.

A SPECIAL PLANET

He loveth righteousness and judgment:
the earth is full of the goodness of the LORD.
PSALM 33:5 KJV

Heavenly Father, the photographs of earth taken from space always cause me to pause because of the stunning beauty they reveal: green forests, brown deserts, white clouds, and blue-green oceans. The earth looks like a marvelous jewel set against the black background of space. It causes me to adore You, Lord, and remember You as the Creator.

Father, I appreciate the earth as Your special creation. Keep me alert to the goodness around me. But help me always be mindful that this earth is not my permanent home. Despite its beauty, the earth is but a way station to a much grander place with You. May I always live my life with the knowledge that heaven is my eventual destination.

Day 362

VICTORY OVER TEMPTATION

How can a young man cleanse his way? By taking heed according to Your word. With my whole heart I have sought You; oh, let me not wander from Your commandments! Your word I have hidden in my heart, that I might not sin against You.

PSALM 119:9–11 NKJV

★ ★ ★

Lord Jesus, I want to be able to say "no" to sin and "yes" to You. But the enemy of my soul throws so many temptations my way. I know I can have victory by storing up the truths of Your Word in my heart. You showed me how that works when You answered the devil's temptation with the Word of God. I know that Your Word is a powerful weapon in my war against sin. Remind me to wield it confidently when the enemy tempts me.

★ A HUMAN SUPPORT SYSTEM ★

Two are better than one, because they have a good return for their labor: If either of them falls down, one can help the other up. But pity anyone who falls and has no one to help them up.

ECCLESIASTES 4:9–10 NIV

Lord, You never intended for me, or any other of Your followers, to make it through life alone. My relationship with You is the most important in my life. But I need the fellowship and companionship with other people—be it with my wife and other family, my friends or fellow church members. I need people in my life who will help pick me up when I'm down, and I desire friends that I can pick up as well. Thank You, Lord, for putting people in my life who act as my support system.

CONFESSION AND CLEANSING

*If we claim to be without sin, we deceive ourselves
and the truth is not in us. If we confess our sins,
he is faithful and just and will forgive us our sins
and purify us from all unrighteousness.*

1 JOHN 1:8–9 NIV

God of righteousness, I've read Your written Word, and I know that all sin is a huge deal to You. You are completely holy and righteous, but You are also merciful and compassionate. I can't earn Your forgiveness, and there's no way I can repay You for it. Loving Father, I admit that I sin. Help me to see my sin as You see it, then bring it to You in confession. Lord, thank You for loving me in spite of my sins and imperfections. Thank You also for forgiving me when I simply confess my sins to You.

═══ WORDS THAT HURT ═══

Out of the same mouth come praise and cursing. My brothers and sisters, this should not be. Can both fresh water and salt water flow from the same spring?

JAMES 3:10–11 NIV

Father, I'm prone to speaking unkind, even harsh, words to and about others. The words I speak matter to You, and I know that You want me to speak only helpful, uplifting words—even when I'm telling another man a needed, painful truth. Please renew my mind daily so that my words toward others are uplifting and kind, not critical and hurtful. When I don't have anything good or helpful to say about another person, help me to hold my tongue. And if I've said anything to hurt another person, help me to seek forgiveness and restoration.

SCRIPTURE INDEX

OLD TESTAMENT

DEVOTIONAL INSPIRATION FOR EVERY MAN!

3-Minute Prayers for Men

This devotional prayer title packs a powerful dose of inspiration into just-right-sized readings for men of all ages and backgrounds. Each of these 180 prayers, written specifically for devotional quiet time, meets you right where you are—and is complemented by a relevant scripture and question for further thought.

Paperback / 978-1-64352-043-8 / $4.99

The 5-Minute Bible Study for Men

In just 5 minutes, you will *Read* (minute 1–2), *Understand* (minute 3), *Apply* (minute 4), and *Pray* (minute 5) God's Word through meaningful, focused Bible study. *The 5-Minute Bible Study for Men* includes more than 90 Bible studies that will speak to your heart in a powerful way.

Paperback / 978-1-64352-274-6 / $5.99